D1314080

JUNIOR DRUG AWARENESS

Nicotine

JUNIOR DRUG AWARENESS

Alcohol

Amphetamines and
Other Stimulants

Cocaine and Crack

Diet Pills

Ecstasy and Other Club Drugs

Heroin

How to Say No to Drugs

Inhalants and Solvents

Marijuana

Nicotine

Over-the-Counter Drugs

Prozac and Other
Antidepressants

Steroids and Other
Performance-Enhancing
Drugs

Vicodin, OxyContin, and
Other Pain Relievers

JUNiOR DRUG AWARENESS

Nicotine

Sean Price

CHELSEA HOUSE
PUBLISHERS
An imprint of Infobase Publishing

Junior Drug Awareness: Nicotine

Copyright © 2008 by Infobase Publishing

Chelsea House
An imprint of Infobase Publishing
132 West 31st Street
New York NY 10001

Library of Congress Cataloging-in-Publication Data

Price, Sean.
  Nicotine / Sean Price.
      p. cm. — (Junior drug awareness)
  Includes bibliographical references and index.
  ISBN 978-0-7910-9696-3 (hardcover)
 1. Nicotine addiction—Juvenile literature. 2. Tobacco use—Juvenile literature.
3. Smoking—Juvenile literature. I. Title. II. Series.

  RC567.P75 2008
  616.86'5—dc22   2007024829

Chelsea House books are available at special discounts when purchased in bulk quantities for businesses, associations, institutions, or sales promotions. Please call our Special Sales Department in New York at (212) 967-8800 or (800) 322-8755.

You can find Chelsea House on the World Wide Web
at http://www.chelseahouse.com

All links and web addresses were checked and verified to be correct at the time of publication. Because of the dynamic nature of the web, some addresses and links may have changed since publication and may no longer be valid.

Text design by Erik Lindstrom
Cover design by Jooyoung An

Printed in the United States

Bang NMSG 10 9 8 7 6 5 4 3 2 1

This book is printed on acid-free paper.

CONTENTS

INTRODUCTION
Battling a Pandemic: A History of Drugs
in the United States   6
by Ronald J. Brogan,
Regional Director of D.A.R.E. America

1   **Why Are People Dying for a Smoke?**   12

2   **How Nicotine Became Popular**   22

3   **The Backlash Against Tobacco**   37

4   **How People Use Nicotine**   53

5   **Nicotine's Impact on Health**   67

6   **Young People and Smoking**   76

7   **Breaking the Nicotine Habit**   86

Chronology   96

Glossary   104

Bibliography   106

Further Reading   110

Photo Credits   114

Index   115

About the Authors   120

Battling a Pandemic: A History of Drugs in the United States

When Johnny came marching home again after the Civil War, he probably wasn't marching in a very straight line. This is because Johnny, like 400,000 of his fellow drug-addled soldiers, was addicted to morphine. With the advent of morphine and the invention of the hypodermic needle, drug addiction became a prominent problem during the nineteenth century. It was the first time such widespread drug dependence was documented in history.

Things didn't get much better in the later decades of the nineteenth century. Cocaine and opiates were used as over-the-counter "medicines." Of course, the most famous was Coca-Cola, which actually did contain cocaine in its early days.

After the turn of the twentieth century, drug abuse was spiraling out of control, and the United States government stepped in with the first regulatory controls. In 1906, the Pure Food and Drug Act became a law. It required the labeling of product ingredients. Next came the Harrison Narcotics Tax Act of 1914, which outlawed illegal importation or distribution of cocaine and opiates. During this time, neither the medical community nor the general population was aware of the principles of addiction.

After the passage of the Harrison Act, drug addiction was not a major issue in the United States until the 1960s, when drug abuse became a much bigger social problem. During this time, the federal government's drug enforcement agencies were found to be ineffective. Organizations often worked against one another, causing counterproductive effects. By 1973, things had gotten so bad that President Richard Nixon, by executive order, created the Drug Enforcement Administration (DEA), which became the lead agency in all federal narcotics investigations. It continues in that role to this day. The effectiveness of enforcement and the so-called "Drug War" are open to debate. Cocaine use has been reduced by 75% since its peak in 1985. However, its replacement might be methamphetamine (speed, crank, crystal), which is arguably more dangerous and is now plaguing the country. Also, illicit drugs tend to be cyclical, with various drugs, such as LSD, appearing, disappearing, and then reappearing again. It is probably closest to the truth to say that a war on drugs can never be won, just managed.

Fighting drugs involves a three-pronged battle. Enforcement is one prong. Education and prevention is the second. Treatment is the third.

Although pandemics of drug abuse have been with us for more than 150 years, education and prevention were not seriously considered until the 1970s. In 1982, former First Lady Betty Ford made drug treatment socially acceptable with the opening of the Betty Ford Center. This followed her own battle with addiction. Other treatment centers—including Hazelton, Fair Oaks, and Smithers (now called the Addiction Institute of New York)—added to the growing number of clinics, and soon detox facilities were in almost every city. The cost of a single day in one of these facilities is often more than $1,000, and the effectiveness of treatment centers is often debated. To this day, there is little regulation over who can practice counseling.

It soon became apparent that the most effective way to deal with the drug problem was prevention by education. By some estimates, the overall cost of drug abuse to society exceeds $250 billion per year; preventive education is certainly the most cost-effective way to deal with the problem. Drug education can save people from misery, pain, and ultimately even jail time or death. In the early 1980s, First Lady Nancy Reagan started the "Just Say No" program. Although many scoffed at the program, its promotion of total abstinence from drugs has been effective with many adolescents. In the late 1980s, drug education was not science based, and people essentially were throwing mud at the wall to see what would stick. Motivations of all types spawned hundreds, if not thousands, of drug-education programs. Promoters of some programs used whatever political clout they could muster to get on various government agencies' lists of most effective programs. The bottom line, however, is that prevention is very difficult to quantify. It is difficult to prove that drug use would have occurred if it were not prevented from happening.

In 1983, the Los Angeles Unified School District, in conjunction with the Los Angeles Police Department, started what was considered at that time to be the gold standard of school-based drug education programs. The program was called Drug Abuse Resistance Education, otherwise known as D.A.R.E. The program called for specially trained police officers to deliver drug-education programs in schools. This was an era in which community-oriented policing was all the rage. The logic was that kids would give street credibility to a police officer who spoke to them about drugs. The popularity of the program was unprecedented. It spread all across the country and around the world. Ultimately, 80% of American school districts would utilize the program. Parents, police officers, and kids all loved it. Unexpectedly, a special bond was formed between the kids who took the program and the police officers who ran it. Even in adulthood, many kids remember the name of their D.A.R.E. officer.

By 1991, national drug use had been halved. In any other medical-oriented field, this figure would be astonishing. The number of people in the United States using drugs went from about 25 million in the early 1980s to 11 million in 1991. All three prongs of the battle against drugs vied for government dollars, with each prong claiming credit for the reduction in drug use. There is no doubt that each contributed to the decline in drug use, but most people agreed that preventing drug abuse before it started had proved to be the most effective strategy. The National Institute on Drug Abuse (NIDA), which was established in 1974, defines its mandate in this way: "NIDA's mission is to lead the Nation in bringing the power of science to bear on drug abuse and addiction." NIDA leaders were the experts in prevention and treatment, and they had enormous resources. In

1986, the nonprofit Partnership for a Drug-Free America was founded. The organization defined its mission as, "Putting to use all major media outlets, including TV, radio, print advertisements and the Internet, along with the pro bono work of the country's best advertising agencies." The Partnership for a Drug-Free America is responsible for the popular campaign that compared "your brain on drugs" to fried eggs.

The American drug problem was front-page news for years up until 1990–1991. Then the Gulf War took over the news, and drugs never again regained the headlines. Most likely, this lack of media coverage has led to some peaks and valleys in the number of people using drugs, but there has not been a return to anything near the high percentage of use recorded in 1985. According to the University of Michigan's 2006 Monitoring the Future study, which measured adolescent drug use, there were 840,000 fewer American kids using drugs in 2006 than in 2001. This represents a 23% reduction in drug use. With the exception of prescription drugs, drug use continues to decline.

In 2000, the Robert Wood Johnson Foundation recognized that the D.A.R.E. Program, with its tens of thousands of trained police officers, had the top state-of-the-art delivery system of drug education in the world. The foundation dedicated $15 million to develop a cutting-edge prevention curriculum to be delivered by D.A.R.E. The new D.A.R.E. program incorporates the latest in prevention and education, including high-tech, interactive, and decision-model-based approaches. D.A.R.E. officers are trained as "coaches" who support kids as they practice research-based refusal strategies in high-stakes peer-pressure environments. Through stunning magnetic resonance imaging (MRI) images, students get to see tangible proof of how various substances diminish brain activity.

Will this program be the solution to the drug problem in the United States? By itself, probably not. It is simply an integral part of a larger equation that everyone involved hopes will prevent kids from ever starting to use drugs. The equation also requires guidance in the home, without which no program can be effective.

Ronald J. Brogan
Regional Director
D.A.R.E America

1

Why Are People Dying for a Smoke?

Until about 1953, smoking **tobacco** was widely viewed as a habit that was smelly but mostly harmless. Scientists had little evidence of a link between tobacco use and disease. Today, we know that **cigarette** smoking is the leading cause of preventable deaths in the United States. More than 438,000 people die each year from smoking-related illnesses. That is more than the annual deaths caused by alcohol, AIDS, drug abuse, murder, suicide, and car accidents combined.

Smokers often admit that their habit is dangerous. Yet, they then shrug and light up another cigarette. British author Peter Taylor recalled the day in 1974 when he and his wife noticed their own ho-hum attitude about smoking. "Like 90% of smokers, we both knew that cigarettes were harmful to health, but we never took the warnings very seriously," he said. "[The warnings] had become part of the furniture, like the cigarette packets themselves."

Why the laidback attitude about a habit that can kill? Perhaps the biggest reason is **nicotine**.

Nicotine is the drug in tobacco that makes smoking a pleasure for some people. It is a stimulant, like cocaine or amphetamines. However, its impact on the body is mild when consumed through one cigarette or wad of **chewing tobacco**. Nicotine also wraps tobacco users in a powerful addiction. Rather than face the painful process of withdrawal, tobacco users keep on smoking or chewing. The Centers for Disease Control and Prevention says that nicotine **addiction** is the most common form of chemical dependence in the United States.

INSIDE A CIGARETTE

A cigarette is made up of chopped-up tobacco leaves wrapped in a thin paper tube. There are several species of tobacco plants. The one used for cigarettes is *Nicotiana tabacum*. As the Latin name indicates, nicotine is a prime ingredient in tobacco.

Until about 500 years ago, tobacco plants were found only in North America and South America. Native Americans smoked and chewed tobacco leaves for centuries before Europeans arrived. White settlers took up the habit and spread tobacco worldwide. Tobacco products are now some of the most commonly used consumer products in the world.

Scientists call a cigarette a "drug delivery system." Its job is to deliver nicotine into a smoker's body. Cigarettes are not the only delivery systems for nicotine. There are also **cigars**, **pipe** tobacco, chewing tobacco, and **snuff**.

The inside of a cigarette is filled with chopped tobacco leaves, blended with chemicals and additives. While many people are aware of the scientifically confirmed link between tobacco and different types of cancer, millions around the world continue to smoke.

Yet, the U.S. tobacco industry produces about 660 billion cigarettes a year, far more than any other tobacco product. That makes cigarettes the primary cause for concern when it comes to nicotine consumption.

Cigarettes contain some surprising ingredients. They include sugar, syrups, licorice, flavorings, and other chemical additives. Most of these additives are designed to make the cigarettes taste better or to help the smoker breathe in the ingredients. The tobacco in cigarettes tends to come from lighter "blends." That means the tobacco leaves have been dried in a smokehouse in such a way as to give them a lighter color. Lighter-colored leaves produce a milder taste. Smokers of pipes, cigars, and other tobacco products usually use darker leaves,

Cigars are made up of outside wrapper leaves, fillers, and binders. The fillers are wrapped-up bunches of leaves inside the wrapper. Those leaves are made of various strengths to produce the main cigar flavor. Binders are elastic leaves that hold together the fillers.

which have a harsher taste. The darker the leaf, the more nicotine is absorbed. An average cigarette contains about 8 or 9 milligrams of nicotine. The average cigar packs about 120 milligrams.

WHO SMOKES?

About 23% of high school students and 8% of middle school students smoke cigarettes. Teen smokers are pretty evenly split between males and females. On top of this, about 10% of high school males and 4% of middle school males use smokeless tobacco.

Many people think of the typical American smoker as a poorly educated 18- to 44-year-old adult who lives below the poverty line somewhere in the South. But

Native Americans and Alaska natives have the highest rate of smoking in the United States, due in part to the use of tobacco in cultural traditions. Here, George Ahmaogak, a former mayor of the Alaskan village North Slope, smokes near a traditional whaling ship.

that doesn't paint the full picture. In all, an estimated 21% of the U.S. population—or 45.1 million people—are smokers. Men tend to smoke more than women: 24% of men and 18% of women are smokers. About 24% of adults aged 18 to 44 smoke. The percentages decrease to 22% of adults between the ages of 45 and 64 and 8.6% of adults aged 65 and older.

About 32% of Native Americans smoke. This is the highest rate of any racial group. Among racial groups, about 26% of whites, 22% of Hispanics, 13% of Asians, and 13% of blacks are currently smokers. Education plays a role in whether someone picks up the cigarette habit. About 43% of adults with only a high school education are smokers. Yet, only about 11% of college graduates

WORLDWIDE SMOKING INCREASES

Efforts to educate people about tobacco in the United States have sparked declines in smoking nationally. Yet, data on smoking trends around the world show that the number of smokers is rising as people in developing countries—including India and China—are warming up to nicotine. More than 15 billion cigarettes are smoked world-wide every day, with tobacco companies manufacturing almost 5.5 trillion cigarettes a year. That's nearly 1,000 cigarettes per every man, woman, and child on the planet.

In 2002, the World Health Organization (WHO) published a report known as *The Tobacco Atlas*. The organization reported that people were lighting up younger, women are the new targets of tobacco marketing, and the manufacturing of cigarettes hit an all-time high.

WHO numbers indicate that there are 1.3 billion smokers in the world, and 84% of those smokers live in developing countries. Demand for cigarettes is high in developing countries mainly because the populations are growing and there is little or no tobacco regulation.

Due to social pressures encouraging youths to smoke, *The Tobacco Atlas* estimates that one-quarter of young smokers have smoked their first cigarette before age 10. Because many of these children are in developing countries where government regulations on cigarette advertisements, access, and taxes are almost nonexistent, the tobacco companies will continue to encourage young people to become new smokers.

(continues on page 18)

(continued from page 17)

While the amount of young smokers is increasing to ensure further consumption in the future, *The Tobacco Atlas* reports that tobacco companies are also concentrating on marketing their products to women in order to make up for a slight decline in male smokers. Cigarette manufacturers have increased production on low-tar, slim, light-colored cigarettes. The mass production of these feminine-looking products and the companies' use of sexy, energetic images to promote their products to women have encouraged at least 250 million females around the world to become smokers in recent years.

light up. Income level also has an impact. About 30% of people living below the poverty line are smokers, while only about 20% of wealthier people are smokers.

TEENAGERS AND SMOKING

Teens need to know about nicotine because each day approximately 4,000 people between the ages of 12 and 17 try smoking for the first time. An estimated 1,140 of these people become regular cigarette smokers. Evidence shows that the younger a person starts smoking, the more likely nicotine addiction will begin.

Almost all of the smokers in the United States started smoking when they were teens. The U.S. **surgeon general**, the nation's top doctor, found that in 1994, 9 of every 10 smokers started smoking before they were 18

FAST FACTS ABOUT NICOTINE

- Worldwide, tobacco use causes nearly 5 million deaths per year.
- Current trends show that tobacco use will cause more than 10 million deaths annually by 2020.
- Cigarette smoking is the leading preventable cause of death in the United States.
- An estimated 38,000 of the 438,000 smoking-related deaths each year are not among smokers. They are caused by **secondhand** smoke exposure.
- For every person who dies of a smoking-related disease, 20 more people suffer with at least one serious illness from smoking.
- Approximately 85% of teenagers who smoke two or more cigarettes probably will become regular smokers.
- People between the ages of 3 and 19 are more likely than older people to live with at least one smoker.
- Nicotine, the key ingredient in tobacco, is as addictive as heroin, cocaine, or alcohol.
- All tobacco products are dangerous. All cause nicotine addiction and all create health problems, including **cancer**.
- Cigarette smoke is more likely to cause lung cancer, while smokeless tobaccos like snuff are more likely to promote mouth and throat cancer.
- On average, smokers die 13 to 14 years earlier than nonsmokers.

(continues on page 20)

(continued from page 19)

Children are the most vulnerable to secondhand smoke because their lungs have not fully developed. Children exposed to smoke at an early age tend to suffer from chronic ear infections, bronchitis, asthma, and even sudden infant death syndrome (SIDS).

- Cigarette smoking increases the length of time that people live with a disability by about 2 years.
- Annually, cigarette smoking costs more than $167 billion, based on lost productivity ($92 billion) and health care costs ($75.5 billion).
- Health care costs associated with secondhand smoke average $10 billion a year.
- In the last 40 years, the percentage of Americans who smoke has dropped by half, to about 21% (about 45.1 million people).
- People who quit smoking, regardless of how old they are when they quit, live longer than those who never quit.

years old, and one-third started before they were 14 years old. By the time these people become adults, about 70% will decide to quit.

Becoming a smoker is a major life decision. As long as a person has no nicotine in his or her system, it is a decision that can be made freely. Once a person starts smoking—even just to experiment—nicotine addiction is likely to skew the decision. Once addicted, people are more likely to accept cigarettes, ignore the warnings, and shrug as they light another cigarette.

How Nicotine
Became Popular

Historians believe that Native Americans may have raised the first tobacco crops as early as 5,000 to 6,000 B.C. By the first century A.D., people in North and South America were chewing dried tobacco leaves or smoking them in pipes. Native Americans used tobacco for pleasure. But the drug also played a key role in many of their religions. The Mayans and the Aztecs included smoking in their ceremonies. The Mayans believed that gods revealed themselves in tobacco smoke.

Christopher Columbus introduced the rest of the world to tobacco after he reached the New World in 1492. At first, though, he wasn't impressed. When Native Americans gave him "certain dried leaves which [give] off a distinct fragrance," Columbus threw them away. Still, within a month or so, Columbus' own Spanish sailors had become hard-core smokers. In the coming decades, Spanish and Portuguese sailors would help spread the habit to other countries.

Columbus took tobacco seeds back to Spain with him, but he never grasped that tobacco could make people rich. Among educated Europeans, only a few scientists showed much interest in the plant. They focused mostly on tobacco's use as a medicine. Around 1561, a Portuguese doctor mentioned tobacco as an amazing new cure-all plant to Jean Nicot, the French ambassador to Portugal. Nicot passed the news on to the French court. People claimed that tobacco cured everything from headaches to bubonic plague. This belief that tobacco actually improved health continued for centuries. During a 1665 outbreak of plague, English schoolboys were beaten if they refused to smoke.

Nicot's name became so tied to tobacco that the plant was given the scientific name *Nicotiana*. From that, we get

WHY IS IT CALLED TOBACCO?

The word *tobacco* probably comes from the word *tobago*. A tobago was the Y-shaped tube that early explorers saw Native Americans use to inhale tobacco smoke. Two prongs of the tobago went into the smoker's nose. They breathed in the smoke from ground-up tobacco leaves. The island of Tobago, part of the Republic of Trinidad and Tobago, is also named after this early pipe.

Tobacco became popular in Europe after Jean Nicot, seen here in a drawing created around 1595, introduced the plant to the Queen of France as a remedy for her headaches. Because of this recommendation, the tobacco plant was given the scientific name of *Nicotiana*.

nicotine, the name of the deadly and addictive chemical found in tobacco. While Nicot pushed tobacco as a medicine among the French, Sir Walter Raleigh promoted it as a source of pleasure among the English. The explorer and adventurer picked up pipe smoking while visiting a friend in North Carolina. Raleigh was a popular figure among English royalty, and his popularity turned smoking into a fad. Even Queen Elizabeth I tried it. But not everyone was happy about smoking. Queen Elizabeth's successor, James I, condemned the habit. He wrote that it is "a custom loathsome to the eye, hateful to the nose, harmful to the brain, [and] dangerous to the lungs. . . ."

TOBACCO SPREADS WORLDWIDE

Several countries, including China and Russia, banned tobacco products for a time. The colony of Massachusetts banned it as well. However, these attacks on tobacco often stemmed more from concerns about fire than health. In an era when most buildings were made of wood, sparks from one pipe could burn down an entire neighborhood or town.

Even with the bans in place, tobacco spread around the globe within 125 years of Columbus' voyage. The rising demand for tobacco turned into a boon for the American colonies. Virginia and the other southern colonies had struggled to attract settlers at first. But within a few years, the profits from tobacco led to a swarm of immigrants from Europe. The crop actually created a labor shortage. Tobacco farmers desperately needed cheap workers to plant and harvest their crops. In 1619, the answer to their prayers landed on the docks at Jamestown, Virginia. Twenty black slaves arrived from Africa—the first of millions to come.

From the 1500s to the early 1800s, most tobacco users either chewed it or smoked pipes. Around 1660, European

LONDON'S VIRGINIA.

The growth of tobacco in colonial Virginia became so profitable that the leaves were used as a form of currency. The heavy demand for tobacco caused Virginia farmers to import slaves from Africa to become cheap laborers. This allowed farmers to grow more and increase profits.

aristocrats launched the snuff craze. Snuff users inhaled a pinch of ground-up tobacco into each nostril. Soon, fashionable young gentlemen began carrying beautifully designed snuff boxes instead of pipes. "Smoking has gone out," one English writer proclaimed.

Then came the French Revolution, which began in 1789. Many French aristocrats were killed or fled overseas. The revolution brought more democratic ideals to France and the rest of Europe. Snuff was linked in people's minds to royalty and repression, and so the snuff craze faded.

During the 1800s, tobacco's popularity kept rising. Cigars became a fashionable way to smoke for rich and poor alike. Pipes and chewing tobacco had always been

TOBACCO AS PAYMENT

Tobacco has served as money many times in history. In pre-Columbian times, Native Americans traded tobacco leaves for valuable goods. This barter system continued long after European colonists arrived. Workers were paid with tobacco and stores accepted it as money. Virginia finally streamlined the process by issuing "tobacco notes" in 1727. The notes, which were used as legal tender, pledged the quality and quantity of a person's tobacco kept in public warehouses. In modern times, tobacco has also been used as money when normal life is disrupted. In post-World War II Europe, for instance, many people did not trust paper money. They needed a money substitute that would be easy to carry, easy to count, and had value. Cigarettes filled that need.

widely used among the lower classes; they finally saw a revival among the rich. In 1839, a North Carolina farmer stumbled upon a new a way to cure, or dry, tobacco leaves. He used charcoal instead of wood. This turned the tobacco leaves a golden color and gave them a mild, buttery taste that smokers enjoyed. This became known as **bright leaf** tobacco.

During the Civil War, both the North and the South used tobacco to fund their efforts. In the tobacco-growing South, tobacco profits helped pay for guns and uniforms. In the North, a **tax** on tobacco raised about $3 million. Both sides issued tobacco as rations to soldiers, a tradition that would continue in later wars. This helped introduce the habit of smoking (or chewing) to thousands. Many Northern soldiers became acquainted with the South's bright leaf tobacco. This created a huge demand for bright leaf tobacco that continued after the war.

THE RISE OF CIGARETTES

The first types of cigarettes were called *cigaritos*. They were leftover scraps of tobacco stems and leaves wrapped in cheap paper. People looked down on them as a poor man's cigar. An Egyptian soldier fighting in Turkey gets credit for inventing the first real cigarette in 1832. His pipe broke, so he began wrapping tobacco in thin paper that was meant to hold gunpowder. His idea caught on with other soldiers, and the idea spread. These cigarettes had to be hand rolled, usually by the smoker himself. By the 1870s, they were still a tiny part of tobacco sales.

More than anyone, James Buchanan "Buck" Duke (1856–1925) made the cigarette the most popular way to use tobacco. Duke was the son of a North Carolina

CHEWING TOBACCO IN CONGRESS

In 1842, English novelist Charles Dickens noted that Americans—especially Southerners—were fond of chewing tobacco. Public buildings had spittoons available to catch the spit from tobacco chewers. Dickens, however, found that U.S. Congressmen were pretty casual about hitting their targets. He reported that carpets in the U.S. Capitol building were covered with tobacco juice. "I strongly recommend all strangers not to look at the floor," he wrote. "And if they happen to drop anything, though it be their purse, not to pick it up with an ungloved hand on any account."

In the past, spittoons were located in public places to prevent people from spitting on the street and reduce the risk of spreading diseases, such as tuberculosis. Chewing tobacco became so popular that even government buildings, including Congressional offices, had spittoons. In this image from 1937, Senator Fred Brown of New Hampshire sits at his desk with a spittoon at his feet.

James Buchanan Duke was the first to mass-produce the cigarette with a special machine. His tobacco company soon became one of the biggest in the United States. It eventually grew to produce up to half of the country's cigarette supply.

tobacco farmer and businessman. (Duke University, in Durham, NC, is named for his family, and he is buried on its campus.)

FIRE SAFETY

Centuries ago, one of the strongest arguments against smoking was that it caused fires. Back then, most buildings and furniture were made of wood and cloth. Today, cigarette-generated fires still destroy billions of dollars worth of property worldwide each year. That's because they usually happen when sleeping smokers drop burning cigarettes onto beds or sofas. About 30% of U.S. deaths from fires—roughly 1,000 people a year—can be blamed on smoking.

A makeshift memorial is constructed outside a house in Bardstown, Kentucky, after 10 people were killed in a fire that started from a lit cigarette. Careless uses of cigarettes have prompted lawmakers to introduce legislation that forces cigarette manufacturers to sell only "fire-safe" cigarettes that can extinguish themselves if dropped or left alone.

TRADING CARDS

Baseball and tobacco have a long history together. Yet, tobacco's most memorable contribution to baseball is probably the trading card. In 1885, tobacco companies began putting small cardboard picture cards in packs to keep the cigarettes from getting crushed. The cards featured many subjects, including animals, actresses, and flags. But the biggest sellers were baseball players. Today, the most valuable baseball card is a 1909 Honus Wagner cigarette card. Wagner opposed smoking and demanded that any cigarette cards with his picture be destroyed. Still, 30 to 50 made it into circulation. A single Honus Wagner card has sold for $2.8 million at auction.

The 1909 Honus Wagner baseball card, originally produced by American Tobacco Company, has become the most valuable baseball card in history. In September 2007, one of the rare cards was sold by auction to a private collector for a record price of $2.8 million. The card was initially created as a marketing ploy to encourage baseball fans to buy and smoke cigarettes.

Duke noticed that the popularity of cigarettes had grown in key places, such as New York City. In 1881, he decided to take a chance on a new machine that could mass-produce cigarettes. The device, invented by James Bonsack of Virginia, could crank out 200 cigarettes a minute. At the time, hand rollers could only make four cigarettes a minute. Duke's gamble paid off.

By 1889, Duke's company was the largest cigarette maker in the United States. Duke soon combined with other cigarette makers. This allowed him to take over U.S. pipe and chewing tobacco sales as well. In 1902, Duke joined forces with English tobacco companies, making his power international.

In 1911, the U.S. Supreme Court ruled that Duke's tobacco empire was a monopoly. That means it had sole control over tobacco in the United States. The court ordered Duke to break the company into five smaller, competing companies: American Tobacco Co., R.J. Reynolds, Liggett & Meyers Tobacco Co., Lorillard, and British American Tobacco. These companies would dominate tobacco sales in the decades to come. Duke made the cigarette even more popular. Yet, by the early 1900s cigarette smokers were still looked down upon. Cigarettes were considered cheap and unmanly. People saw them as a pastime for poor immigrants or workers. That attitude was about to change.

CIGARETTES GO TO WAR

World War I (1914–1918) turned cigarette smoking into a truly national habit. In 1914, cigarettes accounted for only 7% of U.S. tobacco use. By 1920, they accounted for 20%, and were becoming even more popular. By 1922, cigarettes surpassed chewing tobacco as the most consumed tobacco product. More importantly, the war undercut a still strong anti-smoking movement. The

United States entered World War I in April 1917. At that time, cigarette sales were illegal in eight states. Twenty-two states were considering new anti-smoking laws. By war's end, smoking had become too popular for these anti-smoking efforts to succeed.

During the war, tobacco companies handed out millions of free cigarettes to U.S. troops as a morale booster. The goal was to create new customers, and it worked. By one estimate, about 95% of the 1.5 million combat soldiers used tobacco. Cigarettes were easier to carry and light than pipes. They also were less smoky than cigars and less messy than chewing tobacco. Cigarettes quickly lost their reputation for being "not manly enough." Smoking helped soldiers get through the brutal ordeal of combat. A quick smoke could briefly calm frayed nerves while providing a mild pick-me-up. A soldier's life could be tedious as well as terrifying, and smoking gave bored soldiers something to do. "You ask me what we need to win this war," declared Gen. John Pershing, the American commander. "I answer tobacco as much as bullets."

Ironically, before World War I, cigarette smoking was considered unfeminine as well. Women brave enough to smoke did so at home. Police often fined women who were caught in public with cigarettes. Female teachers who smoked could be dismissed from their jobs. This began to change during the 1920s. Movie stars and society women were photographed smoking cigarettes in elegant settings. Popular books, such as Ernest Hemingway's *The Sun Also Rises,* included female smokers. Also, the 1920s was the era of Prohibition, the "Roaring '20s," when all alcohol sales were banned. Illegal bars called speakeasies sprang up to give people places to drink. Women could not only drink forbidden alcohol at speakeasies, but also smoke forbidden cigarettes. Tobacco companies released

Despite the initial social stigma female smokers faced, more women began to smoke cigarettes to signify their independence and sophistication. Tobacco companies began to produce slimmer, longer cigarettes to make them appear fashionable to women smokers. Celebrities, such as actress Rita Hayworth, endorsed cigarettes and encouraged women to smoke specific brands.

new cigarettes designed to be "women's brands." Tobacco ads touted cigarettes as a way to help women stay thin. In 1934, Eleanor Roosevelt became the first First Lady to smoke in public. Even so, female smoking did not gain wide acceptance until World War II broke out in 1939.

Studies made during World War I showed that the tension of war causes tobacco use to rise. During World War II, it jumped so much that tobacco shortages occurred. The United States entered the war in 1941. That year, it was estimated that adult Americans smoked 2,236 cigarettes apiece. By 1945, that number had jumped 54%, to 3,449. Once again, cigarettes were part of soldiers' rations (the share of food and other goods given to them). Charity groups gave away cigarettes to men in uniform. Army training manuals told officers to "smoke and make your troopers smoke." By the end of the 1940s, half of American men and one-third of women smoked. Cigarette sales were at an all-time high.

3

The Backlash Against Tobacco

The turning point in tobacco's popularity came in 1950. That year, five medical studies made the first scientific links between smoking and deadly illnesses. One British study showed that people who smoked heavily were 50 times more likely than nonsmokers to get lung cancer. A U.S. study showed that 95.5% of lung cancer patients were moderate to heavy smokers. Later studies showed other problems. One published in 1957 showed that the children of pregnant smokers were much more likely to be born early, weigh less, and die within one month of birth, compared with children whose mothers did not smoke.

Many smokers greeted this news with indifference or doubt. Other reactions were more complex. The news

(continues on page 40)

CIGARETTES AND HOLLYWOOD

In the 1944 movie *To Have and Have Not*, 19-year-old Lauren Bacall asks, "Anybody got a match?" The actress' smoldering looks and husky voice made it clear that she had more than smoking in mind. Hollywood learned early on that a cigarette could help bring out certain character traits, such as toughness, rebelliousness, or in Bacall's case, sex appeal.

Before 1950, many people smoked, so it was natural that movies showed smoking. But tobacco use declined among the general public starting in the 1950s, while movie characters kept puffing away. The main reason was that tobacco companies paid for product placements. In 1983, for instance, *Rocky* actor Sylvester Stallone took $500,000 from Brown & Williamson in exchange for using the company's products onscreen. Stallone's ad placements never lived up to the ones done on behalf of tobacco company Philip Morris in the 1980 movie *Superman II*. During the movie's climactic battle, Superman takes on alien invaders while flying around and through a series of Marlboro signs.

These product placements were not aimed only at movie audiences. A blockbuster film like *Superman II* would be repeated many times. As one industry document stated in 1981, the idea was to use cigarettes "in such a way that the packages will be readily identified by moviegoers, as well as future cable, television, video cassette, video disc, and network viewers."

Tobacco companies were confident that these placements would get people to smoke. They were right. A series of studies done in the United States, Mexico, and Germany

For decades, tobacco companies have used Hollywood stars to promote their products. Advertisements, such as this one featuring the young and popular actor (and later President of the United States) Ronald Reagan, often ran in popular magazines and newspapers. To further the promotion, the stars were also seen smoking the same brands in their films.

proved it. "The more smoking in the movies kids see, the more they smoke," one researcher at the University of California at San Francisco told Cox News Service in 2006.

Tobacco companies say that they stopped the practice of product placement in the 1990s. Yet critics point out that while smoking among adults has dropped sharply in recent decades, actors still smoke on screen at about the same rate that they did five decades ago. These instances of smoking include children's movies like *101 Dalmatians* (think Cruella De Vil) and those aimed at young teenagers, such as the PG-13-rated *The Fast and the Furious: Tokyo Drift*.

(continues on page 40)

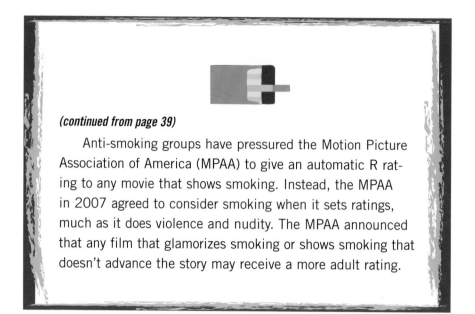

(continued from page 39)

Anti-smoking groups have pressured the Motion Picture Association of America (MPAA) to give an automatic R rating to any movie that shows smoking. Instead, the MPAA in 2007 agreed to consider smoking when it sets ratings, much as it does violence and nudity. The MPAA announced that any film that glamorizes smoking or shows smoking that doesn't advance the story may receive a more adult rating.

(continued from page 37)

that smoking was really, truly harmful seemed to make cigarettes oddly more appealing—especially to teenagers. Hollywood movies already had linked cigarettes with sex appeal and rebelliousness. Also, while smoking was common among adults, adults severely frowned upon children and teenagers smoking. The message to young people was clear: Smoking equaled adulthood and independence.

The generation that came along after World War II—the Baby Boomers—grew up with the smell of cigarette smoke. Grocery stores, offices, restaurants, movie theaters, and hotels allowed smoking. In private homes, it was considered rude to forbid a guest from lighting up. In fact, most non-smoking households had ashtrays on hand for visiting smokers. For the most part, the habit was banned only in areas where it posed a direct danger, such as gas stations and hospitals. Otherwise, schools and houses of worship were the only non-smoking zones in which most children regularly spent time.

Cigarettes were widely accepted in public and private places in the 1950s. People were even allowed to smoke on commercial airplanes, as seen in this photo. Medical studies done in the 1950s confirmed the link between smoking and cancer. Between 1972 and 1990, tougher laws forced the U.S. airline industry to phase out smoking on airplanes.

TOBACCO COMPANIES RESPOND

In December 1953, top tobacco industry officials gathered for a secret meeting at New York's Plaza Hotel. The group's goal was to find a public relations strategy that would counter the damage done by the scientific reports. The aggressive approach they adopted became the model for future battles by the tobacco industry. In the coming decades, the tobacco companies would:

- Deny scientific claims that cigarettes harm people's health, and question those claims directly and through third parties;
- Advertise heavily in ways that countered bad news about cigarettes; and
- Fight against any government restrictions against tobacco products and advertising (when such restrictions became inevitable, they would find ways around them).

In this case, the industry's campaign attacked "the health question" on three different fronts. First, cigarette makers began producing filtered cigarettes. These were soon advertised as being milder and safer than unfiltered brands, even though most studies showed that this wasn't true. Second, the companies supported scientific research designed to show that cigarettes caused little or no cancer risk. Third, the industry moved to counter all claims that smoking was harmful. The industry's main tool was a new group called the Tobacco Industry Research Committee. The group published a booklet quoting 36 scientists who questioned the link between smoking and disease. The booklet and other materials like it were distributed to newspapers, radio stations, and doctor's offices nationwide.

Secretly, the companies' own private scientific research showed what they were keen to deny in public: cigarette smoking causes cancer. In 1953, a researcher for cigarette maker R.J. Reynolds wrote, "Studies of clinical data tend to confirm the relationship between heavy and prolonged tobacco smoking and the incidence of cancer of the lung."

THE SURGEON GENERAL'S REPORT

The momentum against smoking shifted even more dramatically on January 11, 1964. U.S. Surgeon General

U.S. Surgeon General Luther L. Terry presents a report on the connection between smoking and lung cancer to a committee on public health. Shortly afterwards, he established the Surgeon General's Advisory Committee on Smoking and Health. The committee decided the dangers of smoking were so great that the government needed to take immediate action in regulating tobacco and its advertising, which led to the development of the surgeon general's warning on tobacco products.

Luther L. Terry released a bombshell report linking smoking to lung cancer. The 387-page report was titled *Smoking and Health: Report of the Advisory Committee to the Surgeon General of the Public Health Service.*

Dr. Terry had asked some of the nation's top scientists to review all the information available on tobacco's health effects. They concluded that smoking definitely caused cancer in men and probably did in women. The report also stated, "Cigarette smoking is a health hazard of sufficient importance in the United States to warrant appropriate remedial action." In other words, cigarettes needed to be better regulated by the government.

The report's findings have been surpassed by many other studies and reports. We now know for sure that smoking causes cancer in women. Yet, Dr. Terry's report is credited with starting a long-term decline in the number of smokers. By 1970, smoking among men in the United States had fallen to about 37%, well below the 50% seen in the 1950s. The report also started another long-term trend. Since 1964, tobacco companies have been on the defensive, losing ground in the battle for public opinion. Meanwhile, anti-smoking forces have stayed on the offensive and gained greater credibility with the public.

ATTACK AND COUNTERATTACK

Though they were on the defensive, tobacco companies were hardly defenseless. Scientific evidence might pile up against them. Anti-smoking groups might become stronger and more sophisticated. National, state, and local governments might become more aggressive about regulating and taxing tobacco. Yet the tobacco companies still thrived financially. They stuck largely to their aggressive tactics, finding ways to block or counter every attack made against their products.

Tobacco companies were especially good at public relations. They made sure that consumers received conflicting information about the dangers of smoking. A growing number of scientific reports linked smoking to cancer and other health issues. However, books and magazine articles—many of them planted by the tobacco industry—questioned the truth of these studies. For instance, a 1968 *National Enquirer* article stated flatly: "Cigarette Cancer Link is Bunk." Tobacco companies repackaged many of these articles and sent them to doctors nationwide.

In the 1950s and 1960s, most tobacco advertising was done on television. Cigarette ads were a common sight for viewers. Children even saw cigarette ads along with cartoons. By 1970, Congress was set to pass strict rules limiting cigarette advertising. Thus, the companies made a deal with lawmakers. They agreed to stop TV advertising completely. In return, the government agreed that the warning label on cigarette packs would no longer mention cancer. The last televised cigarette ad appeared on December 31, 1970.

This was hardly a setback for the tobacco industry. Without TV ads, companies merely increased advertising in other places, such as billboards and magazines. The companies also found clever ways to get their products seen on television despite the ban. For instance, cigarette brands sponsored sporting events and bought huge signs at sports stadiums that were easily seen by television audiences. "Profits have increased," one tobacco executive wrote in 1976. "The ban on television and other broadcast advertising does not seem to have reduced consumption."

SECONDHAND SMOKE

During the 1970s, anti-smoking groups began focusing on the health dangers of secondhand smoke. In a 1976

PUBLIC HEALTH WARNINGS

One of the biggest changes brought about by the surgeon general's 1964 report was warning labels on cigarette packs. The first warning, which started running in 1965, stated, "Warning—cigarette smoking may be hazardous to your health." A 1984 law decreed that one of four warnings would appear on every cigarette pack (and later print ads). The warnings read:

SURGEON GENERAL'S WARNING: Smoking Causes Lung Cancer, Heart Disease, Emphysema, and May Complicate Pregnancy.

SURGEON GENERAL'S WARNING: Quitting Smoking Now Greatly Reduces Serious Risks to Your Health.

SURGEON GENERAL'S WARNING: Smoking by Pregnant Women May Result in Fetal Injury, Premature Birth, and Low Birth Weight.

SURGEON GENERAL'S WARNING: Cigarette Smoke Contains Carbon Monoxide.

Though well intentioned, these warning labels have done little to discourage smoking. Ironically, they have given tobacco companies immunity to many lawsuits brought by people who have become ill or died because of smoking. The companies claim that these labels give consumers plenty of warning.

lawsuit, a woman successfully sued her employer for not protecting her against cigarette smoke generated by other employees. One tobacco industry report concluded that this line of attack is "the most dangerous development yet to the viability of the tobacco industry that has yet occurred."

The executive was right. Until the issue of secondhand smoke came along, many nonsmokers were blasé about who smoked around them. If other people wanted to smoke, that was their business. But the realization that secondhand smoke was dangerous changed the dynamic of the smoking debate. Smokers could no longer claim to be making an individual choice. By smoking, they were harming the health of those around them.

Now, tobacco companies found it harder to defend their products. Anti-smoking forces gradually saw their efforts pay off on several different fronts:

- In 1973, the U.S. government required airlines to create a non-smoking section on all flights. Smoking was banned in airplane lavatories. By 1990, smoking was banned on all domestic flights lasting six hours or less.
- States and cities began passing stricter laws that banned cigarettes from public places, including private businesses, such as workplaces, restaurants, and bars.
- The federal government, as well as state and local governments, began sharply increasing taxes on tobacco products. They did this because when cigarettes cost more (which happens when taxes go up), people smoke less and are less likely to start smoking.
- A series of new reports by U.S. surgeons general highlighted different aspects of the

dangers of smoking, including a 1994 report that showed smoking's impact on teenagers.

- In 1994, whistleblowers released thousands of once-secret tobacco industry documents. The documents revealed how the tobacco companies suppressed research on the hazards of smoking. They also showed how tobacco companies courted teenagers as "replacement" smokers.

- The news media became more aggressive about covering the tobacco industry. Many news outlets—especially magazines—had been timid about this issue because they were afraid of losing tobacco advertising.

- In 1993, 43% of private U.S. homes banned smoking. By 2003, 75% banned it. The increase was caused largely by better awareness about the dangers of smoking, especially secondhand smoke.

LAWSUITS

Since the 1950s, hundreds of smokers have sued tobacco companies. The smokers are suing for damages caused by smoking-related diseases. None of these suits were successful until 1988. That year, the Liggett Group was ordered to pay Antonio Cipollone $400,000 in damages for contributing to the 1984 death of his wife, Rose. Rose was a long-time smoker. The verdict was later overturned on appeal. The family dropped the case because it was too expensive to continue.

In the 1990s, lawsuits against tobacco companies gained more traction. Many were based on claims that tobacco companies knew nicotine was addictive and deadly but hid that knowledge. These claims were supported by industry documents. During the 1990s, 46 states and five U.S. territories sued the tobacco industry

In 1994, the leaders of the largest U.S. tobacco companies testified before a Congressional committee. The executives denied that their companies manipulated nicotine levels in tobacco products. They also said that tobacco products were not addictive and that they did not believe that smoking caused cancer or other diseases. Few people believed their testimony.

over health care costs tied to smoking. In 1998, the two sides reached a settlement. The industry agreed to pay out $206 billion in exchange for ending all other state claims.

Much of this settlement money was supposed to be spent by the states on anti-smoking programs. However, state lawmakers often spent it in other areas. Yet the settlement won some important concessions from the tobacco industry. They included a prohibition on efforts that target young people, such as the use of cartoon characters in ads. The industry also had to give up outdoor

Phillip Wiley holds a picture of him and his wife on their wedding day as his attorneys stand in the background in February 1998. His wife, Mildred, died of lung cancer after she had worked as a nurse in a hospital where she was constantly surrounded by smoking patients. Wiley sued tobacco companies for failing to inform the public on the dangers of secondhand smoke. In this case, the jury found the tobacco companies not liable for his wife's death.

ads, such as those at sporting events. It could no longer put prominent ads in stores. Tobacco-themed hats, jackets, and other promotional items were banned.

REGULATING TOBACCO

In 1996, President Bill Clinton gave the U.S. Food and Drug Administration (FDA) authority to regulate tobacco. This action would have forced the tobacco industry to follow strict new rules about how it produced, marketed, and sold its products. But the U.S. Supreme Court overturned the president's decision in 2000. The court ruled that current laws did not give the FDA authority over

SMOKERS' RIGHTS

The backlash against smoking has angered some smokers. Many of them see the anti-tobacco movement as something backed by well-meaning zealots. The July-August 2006 *Cigar Aficionado* magazine ran an article that stated:

"The push to prohibit tobacco is being driven by a very small group of very dedicated health nuts. They've been at it now for 40 years, and with the advent of the secondhand smoke issue, they've been able to convince politicians all over America and the world that the only solution is to make it impossible to smoke in public and to charge exorbitant taxes to drive up the cost of tobacco. They refuse to compromise, and have found ever more devious ways to create laws that even prohibit smoking outdoors in some communities."

tobacco. In 2007, Congress began efforts to change that. New bills before Congress would allow the agency to restrict advertising and promotions to children, identify all toxic substances in tobacco products, and require the placement of new and larger warning labels.

4

How People
Use Nicotine

There are three ways to consume tobacco. It can be smoked, chewed, or snorted. Today, most users smoke tobacco. In fact, about 85% of U.S. tobacco is smoked in the form of cigarettes. A cigarette is merely a "nicotine delivery system"—a way to get the highly addictive drug into the body. Cigars, pipes, chewing tobacco, and snuff also are nicotine delivery systems. Each has its own appeal to tobacco users.

CIGARETTES

Early cigarettes had to be hand rolled. Because of that, they were once one of the least popular ways to use tobacco. Smokers could light up a pipe or cigar more easily. Then in the 1880s, tobacco companies started using

Filters were added to cigarettes in the 1950s in an effort to reassure smokers that large amounts of tar and tobacco residue wouldn't reach their lungs. While these filters are highly ineffective, additional ciga-rette filter products have emerged on the market.

machines that could mass-produce cigarettes, making them the cheapest and easiest way to smoke. Heavy advertising and promotion encouraged their use. By the early 20th century, cigarettes had become the dominant form of tobacco use. Cigarettes are so convenient to use that anti-tobacco advocates blame them for boosting the number of people who use tobacco.

Early cigarettes were simply a tube of paper with tobacco inside. In the 1950s, tobacco companies added a filter for the smoker to breathe through. In the United States, these filters are made of cellulose acetate, an absorbent fiber also used in diapers and surgical prod-ucts. These filters are supposed to reduce the level of **tar**, the residue of tobacco smoke that collects in the

BIDIS AND KRETEKS

Some people get hooked on nicotine by smoking **bidis** (*bee-dees*). Bidis come in candy flavors such as chocolate, vanilla, and cherry. They are made of shredded tobacco that's rolled in dried temburni leaves from India. They look cute and are tied up with a string. But bidis deliver far more deadly chemicals to the smoker's lungs than ordinary cigarettes. **Kreteks** (*creh-teks*), which come from Indonesia, are clove-flavored cigarettes. Some people think bidis and kreteks are harmless; they are even sold at some health food stores. Yet, these products are just as dangerous or more dangerous than ordinary cigarettes.

lungs. Filters, however, do little to improve smokers' health. Their main use is actually to keep a cigarette from becoming soggy in a smoker's mouth.

CIGARS

Cigars are made of tobacco leaves wrapped up in a tube shape. Cigars are one of the oldest forms of tobacco consumption. Mayan ruins from A.D. 400–700 have paintings of male figures smoking cigars.

The popularity of cigars has risen and fallen over time. Cigars were extremely popular in the early 1800s and remained so until cigarettes replaced them in the early 1900s. Cigars saw a brief resurgence in the 1960s, and a larger boom in the 1990s. The later fad was fueled in part by the hot-selling luxury magazine *Cigar Aficionado*. Its covers showed actors, athletes, and

Cigars have never been regulated as strictly as cigarettes by the federal government. Whereas cigars were once thought to be for older men, in the 1990s they became more popular among celebrities, athletes, and the general public—including women. Cuban cigars, like the one seen here, are known to be the best-made in the world.

supermodels touting the joys of cigar smoking. Also, trendy cigar bars opened in big cities, and upscale catalogues offered expensive cigar accessories, such as lighters.

Because cigars were not very popular in the mid-1900s, lawmakers placed fewer rules and regulations on them than cigarettes. For instance, cigar boxes and advertisements do not require health warnings in most states. In recent years, tobacco companies have used this loophole to label cigarettes as "little cigars."

Cigar smokers usually do not try to breathe the smoke into their lungs, as cigarette smokers do. Instead, they savor the smoke in their mouths and throats. For that reason, many people believe that cigars are safer than cigarettes. It is true that cigar smokers have a lower risk of lung cancer than cigarette smokers do. Still, a study published in the year 2000 showed that cigar smokers are at least five times more likely to get lung cancer

PRESIDENTIAL PUFFERS

At least 16 U.S. presidents have been serious cigar smokers. Until the early 1970s, cigars were regularly offered
to men after dinner in the White House's Green Room.
Some presidents, such as William McKinley, had to avoid
smoking around their non-smoking wives. But not Andrew
Jackson—his wife, Rachel, liked a good cigar as well.
Ulysses S. Grant was so closely tied to cigars that his
1868 campaign song was "A Smokin' His Cigar." Grant's
habit almost surely contributed to the throat cancer that
killed him in 1885.

than non-smokers. Cigar smokers have the same high
risk as cigarette smokers for cancers in the mouth and
throat. Also, cigar smoke has many more cancer-causing
agents in it than cigarette smoke. Therefore, secondhand
smoke from cigars may be more dangerous.

PIPES

Like cigars, pipes have a long history. Pre-Columbian
Native Americans made them out of clay, wood, bone,
and stone, carving them into elaborate shapes. Pipes
were often holy objects to Native Americans. For Plains
Indians, smoking the Sacred Pipe was a channel to the
spirit world.

Modern pipes have more mundane uses. Most pipes
have a small bowl for holding the tobacco. The smoke
is inhaled through a hollow stem. With water pipes,

Pipes have a bowl to hold the tobacco and a stem for smoking. While pipe smoking is still a part of traditional customs in some cultures, overall pipe smoking has declined over the years.

the smoke is cooled and cleansed as it passes through a small vessel of water.

Pipes' popularity has declined in recent decades. They are widely viewed as stodgy and old-fashioned. But at least one type of pipe—the **hookah**, a kind of water pipe—enjoyed a resurgence in the early 2000s. Hookah bars grew in popularity, especially among the 18- to 24-year-old age group. Many people assume that because the smoke in a hookah is passed through water, it is less dangerous. Yet, research shows that hookah smoke poses the same health hazards as cigarette smoke.

CHEWING TOBACCO

Historians believe that chewing tobacco is the oldest form of tobacco consumption. Native Americans

CHEWING OVER AMERICA'S GAME

Chewing tobacco is as much a baseball tradition as hot dogs and Cracker Jack. In the 1800s, players found that a "chaw" kept their mouths moist on hot summer days. The bull pen, where pitchers warm up, got its name because in the 1860s so many ball players chewed or smoked Bull Durham tobacco. Some of the game's greatest players, including Babe Ruth and "Shoeless" Joe Jackson, played with a lump of chaw in their mouths.

Over time, chewing tobacco's popularity rose and fell among players. In the 1970s, it rose in part because

In the 1950s, Major League baseball player Bill Tuttle (*left*) started chewing tobacco. He continued his habit for 40 years, but stopped when doctors discovered cancerous tumors in his mouth. Tuttle had to have his jaw and cheek removed. He spent the rest of his life urging young baseball players to stop chewing tobacco.

(continues on page 60)

(continued from page 59)

tobacco companies sent free samples of snuff and chewing tobacco to college and professional teams. By 1988, one doctor estimated that at least 300 of the 750 big-league players used smokeless tobacco. By then though, Major League Baseball had begun discouraging tobacco use and banned free samples.

In the 1990s, many teams invited Bill Tuttle to speak to their players. Tuttle had been a third baseman and out-fielder in the 1950s and 1960s, mostly for the Detroit Tigers. He picked up the habit of chewing tobacco as a player and kept it up for nearly 40 years. In 1993, a can-cerous lump in his mouth cost Tuttle his entire jaw and part of one cheek.

Despite reconstructive surgery, Tuttle's face was badly deformed. Tuttle's wife told *The New York Times*, "Million-dollar players would come up with tears in their eyes and a can of tobacco in their hands, and they would say, 'I want you to throw this away for me.'" Tuttle died in 1998.

probably chewed tobacco leaves that were mixed with lime to boost the effects of the drug.

In the 1800s, chewing tobacco was the most popu-lar type of tobacco in the United States. Chewing was simple, cheap, and presented no fire hazard. Also, most Americans were farmers. Chewing allowed them to use tobacco and keep their hands free. For the same reason, chewing tobacco has long been tied to baseball players.

Early types of chewing tobacco were just leaves torn off a plant. U.S. settlers found a way to create a tobacco "**plug**." They sweetened some tobacco with honey and rammed it into holes in maple or hickory logs. Wooden pegs then compressed the tobacco into small cakes. The drying wood soaked up moisture from these cakes, leaving plugs that were ready to consume.

Tobacco chewing declined in popularity during the late 1800s and early 1900s. One reason is that people discovered that spitting spread deadly diseases, such as tuberculosis. Also, cigarettes became much cheaper and easier to use.

SNUFF

Snuff is a powdered form of tobacco that is usually packed with perfumes or flavorings. Dry snuff is sniffed up the nose. Moist snuff is usually "dipped" between the cheek and gum.

In the 1700s, dried snuff was all the rage. There were even schools to show young aristocrats how to inhale snuff properly. After breathing it in, the snuff user usually gave at least one or two hearty sneezes and did some coughing and spitting. All this was considered very healthy. People from all walks of life snorted snuff, making it the most popular form of tobacco consumption for its time. But cigars, pipes, and chewing tobacco had replaced snuff by the early 1800s. Today, most snuff is of the moist variety. Snuff remains a tiny fraction of the tobacco market.

TOBACCO BASICS

Tobacco is the key ingredient in all nicotine delivery systems. The tobacco plant is ordinary looking. It is an annual, meaning it must be replanted every year. A

Roger Quarles, a tobacco farmer in Kentucky, is seen here surveying his crop during a 2005 drought. The federal government stopped subsidizing tobacco farms in 2004, and many farmers stopped growing the crop.

tobacco plant grows about 4 to 6 feet (1.2 to 1.8 m) tall and displays light pink flowers. But it is the 20 or so leaves that are the basis for consumable tobacco.

Tobacco belongs to the genus *Nicotiana*, which is part of a large family of plants that includes potatoes and nightshade. The most common *Nicotiana* species is *Nicotiana tabacum*. It is the tobacco used in all tobacco products. *Nicotiana rustica*, the original species used by Native Americans, has a much higher nicotine content. Some countries use *N. rustica* in tobacco products, though the high nicotine (poison) content also makes it good for pesticides.

Tobacco plants are grown in 21 U.S. states. Most are east of the Mississippi River. Tobacco is an important crop in 60 other countries as well. The United States produces roughly 489,000 tons of tobacco each year. U.S. tobacco production has declined since the 1970s. U.S. products made from tobacco are worth about $25 billion a year. Tobacco taxes are a major source of income for the U.S. government, as well as state and local governments.

PLENTY OF TOBACCO PLANTS

Check out where tobacco grows around the world.

TOP FIVE TOBACCO-GROWING COUNTRIES*	
China	2.6 million tons
Brazil	660,000 tons
India	582,000 tons
United States	489,000 tons
Zimbabwe	220,000 tons

Source: Food and Agriculture Organization of the United Nations

TOP FOUR TOBACCO-GROWING STATES*	
North Carolina	191,000 tons
Kentucky	127,000 tons
Tennessee	42,000 tons
South Carolina	36,500 tons

Source: U.S. Department of Agriculture
*Three-year average, 2000–2002 data

TYPES OF TOBACCO

There are many ways to classify tobacco. Most experts look at the way in which the tobacco leaves are cured, or dried, once they are picked. The tobacco is also left to age and ferment, like wine. The curing and fermenting process creates important chemical changes that remove bitterness and improve the flavor of the leaves. There are three main types of tobacco used in cigarettes.

- *Bright leaf (or flue-cured or Virginia)*—This type of tobacco is dried in barns using heat that radiates from pipes, or flues. Bright leaf gets its name because the process tends to lighten the color of the leaves. It also results in a mild tobacco that is easier to inhale.
- *Burley*—This air-cured tobacco was discovered in 1864 when an Ohio farmer found he was growing a mutant strain of the plant. **Burley** quickly became popular, in part because of its ability to absorb artificial sweeteners such as licorice.
- *Oriental*—**Oriental** gets its name because it is grown mainly in Turkey and other parts of Asia. It is cured in the sun and has a famously harsh smell.

Farmers pick tobacco leaves mostly by hand. Each year, hundreds of tobacco field workers come down with "green tobacco sickness." It is caused by an overdose of nicotine from contact with tobacco leaves. The nicotine is absorbed through the skin and even soaks into clothes. Among other things, green tobacco sickness causes nausea, vomiting, dizziness, and a rapid heartbeat. It can make people feel sick for days.

Monte Holley, seen here checking his crop, grows Burley tobacco in Virginia. Burley is a specific type of tobacco that is air-cured and flavored with sweeteners. It is usually grown in Kentucky, Ohio, Indiana, and West Virginia.

After picking, many types of tobacco are cured to create a darker leaf color. These are used in pipe tobacco, cigars, chewing tobacco, and snuff. In all of these products, companies tend to mix different tobaccos together to create a variety of flavors. But tobacco is not the only thing that provides flavor. Each cigarette contains 599 additives and preservatives. In fact, a cigarette is about 10% additives by weight.

Many additives include harmless-sounding things such as cocoa and licorice. But those substances work in unusual ways when burned. For instance, cocoa and licorice contain chemicals that relax the bronchial muscle, allowing the smoker to breathe the smoke in deeper. The addition of sugar offsets the natural bitterness of tobacco and reduces irritation caused by the smoke. **Menthol** gives cigarettes a minty flavor. Other additives help preserve the tobacco in the pack or help control the rate at which it burns. All of them are geared toward making smoking more pleasant and more addictive.

WHO SELLS TOBACCO?

Large tobacco companies have a hold on U.S. and international markets. Look how these companies stack up:

Percentage of the world market
China National Tobacco Company—31% (China has almost 400 million smokers)
Altria (formerly Philip Morris)—17%
British American Tobacco (BAT)—13%
R.J. Reynolds—6%
Rothmans International—4%

Percentage of the U.S. market
Altria (formerly Philip Morris)—50%
R.J. Reynolds—24%
Brown & Williamson (B&W)—13%
Lorillard Tobacco—10%
Liggett Group—1%

Source: Associated Press, July 14, 2000

5

Nicotine's Impact on Health

Nobody plans to become addicted to nicotine. Yet, in most cases, nicotine addiction is bound to happen to anyone who regularly uses tobacco. Nicotine's power can be seen in the way just one cigarette affects a smoker. An ordinary cigarette contains only about 8 or 9 milligrams of nicotine (there are about 28,000 milligrams in 1 ounce). Of that, the smoker actually inhales only about 1 to 1.5 milligrams. Yet, that is more than enough to cause addiction and change body chemistry.

HOW NICOTINE WORKS
Nicotine is an alkaloid, an organic compound that contains carbon, hydrogen, nitrogen, and oxygen. Alkaloids are used as medicines, illegal drugs, and poisons. For

instance, the poppy plant produces the helpful pain killer codeine and the highly addictive drug opium. Tiny amounts of nicotine produce the brief rush of pleasure that smokers feel when they light up. Larger amounts of nicotine are lethal enough to be the active ingredient in bug sprays.

Nicotine is just one of many toxic chemicals found in tobacco smoke. However, nicotine is the chief reason that smokers find their habit irresistible. With every puff, tiny amounts of nicotine spread out into the lungs. Blood enters the lungs to pick up oxygen. When it does, nicotine becomes absorbed into the blood as well. The heart pumps the blood to all parts of the body. A smoker who eagerly inhales cigarette smoke feels the effects of the drug when nicotine-laden blood reaches his or her brain. That journey takes about 5 to 10 seconds.

Neurotransmitters send chemical messages from the brain to the rest of the body. Once the nicotine reaches the brain, it triggers the release of certain key neurotransmitters. **Adrenaline** (also called epinephrine) causes the release of glucose (sugar). This increases the heart rate, breathing rate, and blood pressure. **Dopamine**, a chemical in the brain, is released at times of pleasure. If you're petting a kitten or having a fun afternoon with a friend, dopamine is the reward. Nicotine boosts dopamine as well. Other addictive drugs, such as cocaine, also increase dopamine.

First-time smokers seldom have a fun experience. The smoke causes them to gag and cough. The sudden appearance of so much nicotine in the brain makes them feel dizzy and sick. Headaches are common. But other factors—such as peer pressure or curiosity—can override these warnings from the body. With repeated exposure, the body finds the presence of nicotine normal and the absence of nicotine abnormal. Over time, the smoker needs to have more nicotine to get the same high felt with those first cigarettes. Without nicotine, a smoker's dopamine levels decline. Within minutes of finishing a cigarette, a smoker starts to feel stressed, anxious, and depressed. Therefore, he or she lights up another cigarette, and the cycle begins again.

People who use smokeless tobaccos follow a similar path to addiction by absorbing the nicotine through their skin. Their risk of addiction is slightly lower than that of smokers because smoking creates a faster, more

CHEMICAL STEW

Tobacco smoke is a witch's cauldron of more than 4,000 chemicals. About 60 are known to cause cancer. Here's a list of some of the chemicals in tobacco smoke, and where else you can find them.

Acetone—paint stripper
Ammonia—floor cleaner
Arsenic—ant poison
Butane—lighter fluid
Cadmium—car batteries
Carbon monoxide—car exhaust
DDT—insecticide
Hydrogen cyanide—gas chambers
Methanol—rocket fuel
Naphthalene—mothballs
Toluene—industrial solvents
Vinyl chloride—plastics

powerful nicotine rush. However, all tobacco products contain enough nicotine to cause addiction.

WHY YOUNG SMOKERS SHOULD WORRY

Every cigarette that a smoker consumes takes away seven minutes of his or her life. This backward countdown seems like a remote problem to teenage smokers. Many assume that they'll quit smoking before any health problems arise. They also assume that health problems happen only after decades of smoking. That is not true.

New smokers usually find that breathing has become more difficult, especially when they try to exercise or do physical work. That is because tobacco use reduces the amount of oxygen that the blood can carry. Nicotine also

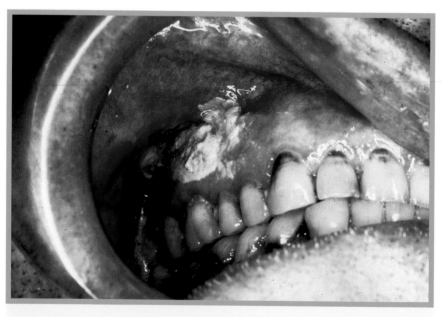

Smoking and chewing tobacco not only stain your teeth and gums, they also cause enamel loss in teeth and cancer. This image shows how tobacco use has caused teeth and gum discoloration as well as a large, pre-cancerous lesion known as leukoplakia.

LIGHT CIGARETTES NOT HEALTHIER

When people began to complain about the health effects of cigarettes, tobacco companies developed a new product touted as a safer alternative—the "light" or "low tar" cigarette. Smokers believed that they were doing less damage to their bodies and lungs by smoking cigarettes with less nicotine and tar.

Various studies between 2001 and 2007 have shown, however, that light and low tar cigarettes are not, in fact, safer than regular cigarettes. Smokers are still inhaling the same amount of hazardous chemicals as they would have when smoking an ordinary cigarette, and they have the same high risk of developing various types of cancer, heart problems, and diseases. Currently, 45% of smokers smoke light cigarettes and are less likely to quit than those who smoke regular cigarettes.

Tobacco companies manufacture light cigarettes by putting microscopic holes into the filters. They say their researchers have found that air allowed inside the cigarette would dilute the smoke before it entered a smoker's lungs. Scientists, however, found that people often take longer and deeper drags (inhales) on light cigarettes, which draws more toxic chemicals into their body than they would with a normal cigarette. Also, the tiny holes located in the filter of light cigarettes actually block out the air they were supposed to enable smokers to draw in while smoking.

First sold in the late 1960s, light and low tar cigarettes were marketed to people (particularly women) by highlighting their mild, smooth flavor. While the consumer may not

(continues on page 72)

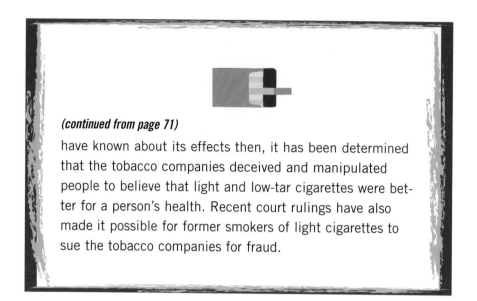

(continued from page 71)

have known about its effects then, it has been determined that the tobacco companies deceived and manipulated people to believe that light and low-tar cigarettes were better for a person's health. Recent court rulings have also made it possible for former smokers of light cigarettes to sue the tobacco companies for fraud.

speeds up a smoker's heart rate. Both leave the smoker panting for breath, even during minor exercise. In young people, smoking can cause breathing-related illnesses. It also can make colds and asthma more serious.

Tobacco use also is hard on a smoker's mouth. Cigarettes and smokeless tobacco stain teeth and gums, and they create bad breath. Tobacco users are at higher risk for tooth decay and gum disease. Smokeless tobacco can cause lesions on the mouth and tongue.

The gum problems and tooth decay may not crop up during the teenage years. But they can become a problem once smokers reach their 20s or 30s. Saving or replacing teeth that have been undermined by smoking is expensive. Plus, if a person is still smoking after his or her teeth are fixed, the problems will continue.

Also, within just a few years of picking up the habit, smokers begin to see aging in their skin. "Smoker's face" occurs because smoking breaks down the body's ability to replace old skin cells with new ones. Wrinkles appear around the mouth and eyes. The skin also starts to look grayish. This premature aging gets worse as long as the smoker keeps smoking.

LONG-RANGE HEALTH PROBLEMS

In the early 1900s, lung cancer was a rare disease. It made up less than 5% of all cancers. But there was a sudden surge in cigarette smoking that began in the 1910s and 1920s. This caused lung cancer rates to soar by the 1950s. Today, lung cancer is the most common cancer in the world. It accounts for about one-third of all cancer deaths. In 2003, lung cancer killed more than 158,000 Americans. Smoking is responsible for 90% of lung cancer cases.

Lung cancer is not the only lung-related problem tied to smoking. Emphysema affects about 3.1 million Americans each year. The disease makes lungs less elastic. This makes it difficult to breathe. About 80% to 90% of all deaths from emphysema are tied to smoking.

Tobacco smoke also attacks the heart. Cardiovascular conditions—mainly heart attacks and strokes—are the top killer in the world. In 2005, they were responsible for 30% of all deaths worldwide, which is about 17.5 million deaths. The three major causes of heart problems are an unhealthy diet, lack of physical exercise, and tobacco use.

Tobacco use affects every organ of the body. Here is a brief list of some of the other conditions caused by smoking:

- Many cancers, including leukemia and cancers of the mouth, throat, and liver
- Weakened immune system
- Lung problems, such as chronic bronchitis
- Slower healing of wounds

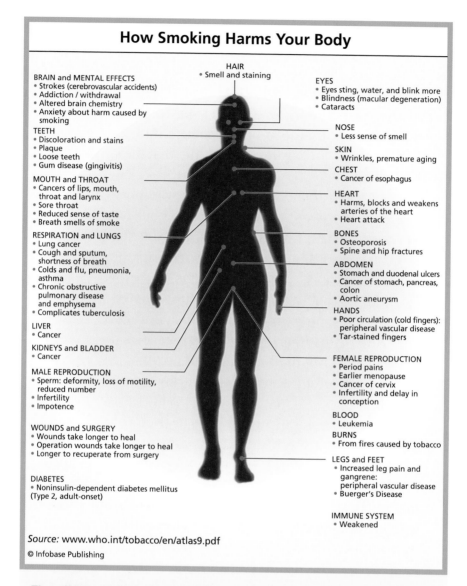

How Smoking Harms Your Body

HAIR
• Smell and staining

BRAIN and MENTAL EFFECTS
• Strokes (cerebrovascular accidents)
• Addiction / withdrawal
• Altered brain chemistry
• Anxiety about harm caused by smoking

TEETH
• Discoloration and stains
• Plaque
• Loose teeth
• Gum disease (gingivitis)

MOUTH and THROAT
• Cancers of lips, mouth, throat and larynx
• Sore throat
• Reduced sense of taste
• Breath smells of smoke

RESPIRATION and LUNGS
• Lung cancer
• Cough and sputum, shortness of breath
• Colds and flu, pneumonia, asthma
• Chronic obstructive pulmonary disease and emphysema
• Complicates tuberculosis

LIVER
• Cancer

KIDNEYS and BLADDER
• Cancer

MALE REPRODUCTION
• Sperm: deformity, loss of motility, reduced number
• Infertility
• Impotence

WOUNDS and SURGERY
• Wounds take longer to heal
• Operation wounds take longer to heal
• Longer to recuperate from surgery

DIABETES
• Noninsulin-dependent diabetes mellitus (Type 2, adult-onset)

EYES
• Eyes sting, water, and blink more
• Blindness (macular degeneration)
• Cataracts

NOSE
• Less sense of smell

SKIN
• Wrinkles, premature aging

CHEST
• Cancer of esophagus

HEART
• Harms, blocks and weakens arteries of the heart
• Heart attack

BONES
• Osteoporosis
• Spine and hip fractures

ABDOMEN
• Stomach and duodenal ulcers
• Cancer of stomach, pancreas, colon
• Aortic aneurysm

HANDS
• Poor circulation (cold fingers): peripheral vascular disease
• Tar-stained fingers

FEMALE REPRODUCTION
• Period pains
• Earlier menopause
• Cancer of cervix
• Infertility and delay in conception

BLOOD
• Leukemia

BURNS
• From fires caused by tobacco

LEGS and FEET
• Increased leg pain and gangrene: peripheral vascular disease
• Buerger's Disease

IMMUNE SYSTEM
• Weakened

Source: www.who.int/tobacco/en/atlas9.pdf
© Infobase Publishing

The effects of long-term smoking and tobacco intake are devastating to the human body.

- Blindness
- Loss of smell and taste
- Early menopause in women

- Psoriasis, a disease that affects the skin and joints
- Osteoporosis, or thinning of the bones
- High blood pressure
- Impaired fertility in men and women
- Birth defects

HEALTH EFFECTS OF SECONDHAND SMOKE

Smoking does not endanger only smokers. In the 1970s and 1980s, scientists began showing that secondhand, or passive, tobacco smoke was harmful. There are two types of secondhand smoke: exhaled and sidestream. Exhaled smoke comes from a smoker. Sidestream smoke comes from the burning end of the cigarette. Of the two, sidestream smoke is more harmful. Exhaled smoke has been filtered through the smoker's lungs, removing some of the deadly chemicals. Also, sidestream smoke is made while the cigarette is not being puffed. That means the tobacco burns at a lower temperature, which releases more harmful compounds into the air.

Each year in the United States, exposure to second-hand smoke is estimated to cause at least 3,000 deaths from lung cancer and 35,000 to 62,000 adult deaths from cardiovascular diseases. Secondhand smoke is a special worry for young children. It can increase the risks for asthma and bronchitis, fluid in the middle ear, and sudden infant death syndrome (SIDS). Pregnant women exposed to secondhand smoke are more likely to have underweight babies.

6

Young People and Smoking

Each day, more than 1,172 Americans die from smoking-related illnesses. Trying to replace these customers might be a crisis for tobacco companies. But the companies have found a reliable pool of replacements: children and teens. In 1984, a researcher for R.J. Reynolds summed up the industry's dependence on the under-18 crowd: "If younger adults turn away from smoking, the industry will decline, just as a population which does not give birth will eventually dwindle."

WHY DO YOUNG PEOPLE SMOKE?

Today, about one-quarter of teenagers smoke. Almost all adult smokers—90%—started before they turned 18. Oddly, many teenagers today know all about the dangers of smoking, yet decide to smoke anyway. The reasons for this are as complex as each smoker's personality, but there are some common thoughts behind their behavior.

Quitting Will Be Easy

Almost every teenager who starts smoking thinks it will be easy to stop. According to the American Cancer Society, only about 3 out of 100 high school smokers believe that they still will be smoking in 5 years. But in fact, most of them will be. It takes an average of 16 to 20 years between the time a smoker first tries to quit and when he or she actually is able to successfully quit. By then, many have already irreversibly damaged their health.

Parents Do It

Many people assume that teenagers learn to smoke from watching their parents. But research on the subject is mixed. Some studies say yes, and others say no. Yet, having a parent who smokes definitely creates opportunities for teenagers to experiment with smoking. Cigarettes are often left around the house and easily can be stolen. Also, a parent who smokes is not in a strong position to discourage children from smoking.

Friends Do It

Four out of five teenagers who smoke lit up their first cigarettes with friends, siblings, or someone else they knew. Studies also show that teenagers are much more likely to smoke if a best friend does. Teenagers who smoke tend to have lower self-esteem and lower grades than others. They tend to be teens whose parents have divorced, or who come from poorer families or from families with serious problems. All this makes these teens more susceptible to peer pressure. Research shows that smoking often is the first step toward using alcohol and illegal drugs. Drug use in general (including smoking) makes many teenagers feel accepted at parties, dances, and in other social situations.

Bucking Authority

Teenagers are famously rebellious. For many of them, smoking is worth trying because parents, teachers, coaches and other adults agree that it's bad. Teenagers also are much more likely than adults to take risks.

 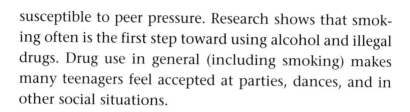

EASY ADDICTION

Many young people don't believe they will become addicted to nicotine with the very first puff, but a recent study has shown that the opposite is true: your first puff can leave you hooked for life.

Between 2002 and 2006, researchers interviewed and tracked the smoking habits of a group of sixth graders in Massachusetts who had inhaled at least once while smoking a cigarette, and found that almost 60% of these students lost control of the amount of their smoking, while 38% of them developed a dependency on tobacco. Those who became dependent on cigarettes experienced changes in their mood, as well as cravings, a desire to smoke, and an inability to quit.

While some people believe that smoking is a psychological habit, researchers also discovered that 91% of the students in the study group who experienced feelings of

Unfortunately, at least half the young people who continue to smoke as adults will die early because of the habit. Others will struggle for years to quit.

Losing Weight

Many smokers—especially girls and women—start smoking to help control their weight. Certain brands names, such as Virginia Slims, even play off the belief that cigarettes are a kind of smokeable diet pill.

Smoking sometimes helps people eat less because the hand-to-mouth activity of smoking distracts them from

relaxation from smoking their first cigarette began to smoke regularly and admitted that they were unable to stop. This finding may shift the belief that the main reasons young people smoke are not just social and personality-related reasons, such as peer pressure and rebelliousness, but also biological causes that make it harder to quit.

The Massachusetts study, published in the October 2007 issue of the journal *Pediatrics*, currently is being debated among scientists. The researchers themselves admit that this study does not include many outside factors, such as puberty and alcohol or drug use. Yet, the results provide further insights into the research and study of addiction and smoking.

"People used to think that long-term heavy use caused addiction," said Dr. Joseph DiFranza, lead author of this research project. "Now, we know it's the other way around: addiction is what causes long-term heavy use."

the hand-to-mouth activity of eating. Also, smoking does raise the body's metabolic rate slightly. This means smokers burn more calories. However, smokers tend to store fat on the waist and torso, rather than on their hips. This puts them at greater risk of heart disease, diabetes, and other health problems. Studies have found that when smokers quit, they do eat more, though the average weight gain is only about five pounds (2.27 kg).

Other research has shown that smokers eat more than non-smokers do, and that smokers tend to eat more junk food. Many people trying to lose weight by smoking end up with the worst of all worlds. They do not lose weight, and they become addicted to nicotine. The only sure, safe way to lose weight is to eat healthy foods and get plenty of exercise.

Easing Stress

Teenagers lead stressful lives. Adolescent bodies change rapidly, and many teenagers live with intense pressure to make good grades and fit in at school. Cigarettes seem to relieve some of this stress. But any relief they bring is temporary, and they bring a new set of health worries. Also, cigarettes do not address a person's underlying problems. Many teens who smoke are depressed. Light smokers are five to six times more likely than non-smokers to attempt suicide. Heavy smokers are 18 times more likely.

Looking Good in Movies

Many teenagers overestimate how many smokers really exist. That misperception stems in part from the way smokers are represented in movies and on TV. For instance, the number of young adults shown smoking on camera more than doubled between the 1960s and the 1980s. That happened even as the number of U.S. smokers fell by 17%. Movies that show a lot of smoking shape attitudes. One 2001 study by Dartmouth University researchers found that the more instances of smoking that young people saw in movies, the more likely they were to try smoking themselves.

ADVERTISING PLAYS A ROLE

In 2005, tobacco companies spent more than $13 billion—about $36 million per day—promoting their products. The companies have argued for decades that their ads and promotions do not target young people. These claims have been met with great skepticism, in part because the companies' own documents show just the opposite. For instance, once-secret memos and letters

Joe Camel became one of the most recognizable images connected to cigarettes in the late 1980s and early 1990s. The federal government and anti-tobacco groups forced Joe Camel into retirement, claiming that the advertisements featuring the cartoon smoking camel were geared toward children.

obtained from Brown and Williamson reveal that the company has courted teenagers aggressively, looking for subtle ways to link cigarettes with marijuana, beer, wine, and sex.

THE STEPS TO SMOKING

Researchers have found that teenagers go through a series of identifiable steps on their way to becoming smokers. These steps usually take place gradually over several months or years.

Laying the groundwork: Though no smoking takes place, a young person is exposed to smoking from parents, movies, ads, and other sources.

Trying it out: Curiosity leads to trying one or two cigarettes.

Experimenting: Smoking takes place occasionally, but there is no intention of becoming a smoker.

Regular smoker: Smoking takes place once a month or maybe once a week, but there is still no daily smoking.

Daily smoker: Smoking takes place on most days. This person is now addicted to nicotine.

Source: Adapted from Mayhew, K.P, BR. Flay, and J.A. Mott, "Stages in the Development of Adolescent Smoking," Drug and Alcohol Dependence 59, Supp. 1 (2000) S61-S81.

Tobacco company ads almost uniformly make smoking look like a fun activity. The smokers they show are almost always good-looking, independent 20-somethings—exactly the type of people most teenagers long to be. Perhaps the most famous tobacco advertising campaign revolved around the cartoon character Joe Camel. R.J. Reynolds launched this ad campaign in 1988 to promote Camel cigarettes. The company denied repeatedly that Joe Camel was aimed at children or teenagers. Yet studies showed that Joe Camel had become as recognizable to 6-year-olds as Mickey Mouse.

After intense criticism, R.J. Reynolds agreed to stop using the Joe Camel character in 1997. In recent years, tobacco companies have launched advertising campaigns that at least appear to be discouraging children from smoking. One of them encourages young people to "Think. Don't smoke." Others remind young people that they have to be 18 to buy tobacco products. Anti-tobacco groups criticize the ads as being totally ineffective while reinforcing the message that smoking is an adult activity. Critics believe the ads exist only so that tobacco companies can argue in court cases that they have at least tried to discourage underage smoking.

ANTI-SMOKING ADS WORK

In 1998, tobacco companies reached a $206 billion legal settlement with 46 states and 5 U.S. territories over the health impact of cigarettes. A small portion of that money was dedicated to pay for a nationwide advertising campaign designed to cut youth smoking rates.

The American Legacy Foundation ran the "Truth" ad campaign. The foundation asked teens their opinions on the most effective ways to dampen interest in smoking. They found that teenagers dislike the idea that tobacco companies are manipulating them. So many "Truth"

Efforts to discourage smoking have led to public education campaigns, including the one seen here. These warnings, used on cigarette packages by the European Union, are meant to raise awareness about the health hazards of smoking.

ads play up the ways in which tobacco companies have misled the public.

The "Truth" campaign also looked for creative ways to illustrate the health problems linked with cigarettes. One ad featured a rugged-looking cowboy. After the man gets off his horse, he removes a bandana to reveal a wound at the base of his throat. Then, with the help of a mechanical voice device, the cowboy sings:

"You don't always die from tobacco,
Sometimes you just lose a lung
Oh, you don't always die from tobacco
Sometimes they just snip out your tongue.
And you won't sing worth a heck
With a big hole in your neck
Cuz you don't always die from tobacco."

The ad then flashes a sign that says, "Over 8.5 million Americans live with tobacco-related illnesses."

Between 1997 and 2002, teen smoking rates fell from 28% to 18%. The *American Journal of Public Health* credited the Truth ads with about one-fifth of that drop. Unfortunately, the money for the ads largely dried up in 2003. The ads still run on cable television programs aimed at young people, though the American Legacy Foundation now makes fewer of them.

SELLING TOBACCO TO MINORS

Since the early 1900s, states have had laws on the books that ban the sale of tobacco to minors. However, those laws have largely been winked at by stores and by teenagers. In 1987, one researcher found that an 11-year-old girl bought tobacco successfully in 75 out of 100 attempts. In 1992, a federal law forced all states to forbid the sale of tobacco to people younger than 18 years of age. But enforcement by states remains erratic. Thousands of teenagers still find ways to get tobacco.

7

Breaking the Nicotine Habit

"It's easy to quit smoking; I've done it lots of times." That old joke says a lot about how hard it is to stop smoking (or chewing or dipping). Quitting is hard in part because of nicotine's impact on the body. Nicotine changes the way the brain and other organs function. Tobacco use also changes the way food tastes and the way things smell. The body becomes used to having nicotine. When the body stops getting nicotine, stress levels rise sharply.

Smoking is just as addictive psychologically as it is physically. The habit of smoking becomes ingrained in daily routines. Smokers get used to having a cigarette with breakfast or after class. They enjoy sharing a cigarette while they talk with friends. Changing these day-to-day activities can be as hard to cope with as the physical withdrawal.

WHY QUIT?

Giving up nicotine is so hard that most tobacco users need compelling reasons to quit. Here are just a few.

Better Health

About half of all smokers who don't quit will die from a smoking-related illness. Most will die of heart disease, emphysema, or lung cancer. Others will die in fires set by their own cigarettes. Secondhand smoke endangers others as well.

Smell and Appearance

Smokers carry the aroma of stale cigarette smoke around everywhere they go, though most can no longer smell it themselves. This smell is in their clothes, hair, cars, backpacks, and rooms. Smokers have bad breath, too. Plus, cigarettes discolor teeth, fingers, and fingernails.

Social Acceptance

Increasingly, the world is becoming a no-smoking zone. In the United States, there has been a sharp rise in the number of smoking bans at workplaces, malls, restaurants, bars, and even private homes. That means smokers must find an outdoor spot to smoke, no matter what the weather is like.

Saving Money

In 1999, U.S. smokers paid just under $3 for one pack of cigarettes. Today, each pack costs about $4. The cost will continue to rise. Prices naturally rise over time, and governments are now imposing larger taxes on tobacco products. The $28 a week that a pack-a-day smoker pays for cigarettes adds up to $1,456 a year. Smokers also pay more for health insurance and life insurance.

HOW TO QUIT

There are many ways to approach quitting. One is to simply go "cold turkey": stop buying cigarettes and use willpower to fight off cravings. This approach works for some smokers. But most need more preparation to make such a radical change. Whether you are trying to quit yourself or helping a friend, try to keep these steps in mind.

Get Ready

The first step is to decide to quit. Once smokers come to that conclusion, they need to study their own habits. Consider: When do they smoke? What times do they enjoy it the most? With whom do they smoke? How will friends react? Preparing for these moments makes a relapse less likely.

After that, it is important to choose a quitting date. Find a date when stress levels will be relatively low. Quitting smoking is difficult. Any effort to quit right before a major test or important performance is likely to fail.

Also, get rid of all cigarettes, ashtrays, and other items that make smoking convenient. At the same time, buy substitutes such as sugarless gum to keep the mouth busy.

Find Support

Smokers should tell friends and family that they plan to quit. Let them know when the quit date is and remind them as the day gets near. Those trying to quit should also ask smokers to be polite and not smoke around them. Ask ex-smokers about their experiences. They may have insights that can help.

RESOURCES FOR HELP AND INFORMATION

The following organizations can provide people with information about tobacco and quitting smoking.

American Cancer Society
This nonprofit group offers information on health risks tied to tobacco use and resources for preventing and coping with cancer.
1-800-ACS-2345 (1-800-227-2345)
http://www.cancer.org

American Heart Association
This organization provides materials designed to educate the public about heart disease, including tobacco-related illnesses. AHA also offers programs designed to help end smoking at schools and workplaces.
1-800-AHA-USA1 (1-800-242-8721)
http://www.americanheart.org

American Lung Association
This organization offers valuable resources that highlight the many ways in which tobacco products endanger healthy lungs.
1-800-548-8252 (1-212-315-8700)
http://www.lungusa.org

Campaign for Tobacco-Free Kids
This group educates children and teenagers about tobacco issues and encourages them to become actively involved in combating nicotine addiction.
1-202-296-5469
http://www.tobaccofreekids.org

(continues on page 90)

(continued from page 89)

Centers for Disease Control and Prevention (CDC)
One of the U.S. government's major health research agencies offers a wide range of information on tobacco-related issues.
1-770-488-5705
http://www.cdc.gov/tobacco

National Cancer Institute
The NCI, part of the U.S. Department of Health and Human Services, offers programs and publications that inform people about smoking and show them ways to quit.
1-800-4-CANCER (1-800-422-6237)
http://www.cancer.gov

World Health Organization
WHO is the health arm of the United Nations. It offers a wide array of information about tobacco and its global impact.
011-41-22-791-2126 (International call to Switzerland)
http://www.who.int/tobacco/en/

Find Resources

Some people prefer to stop smoking on their own. Others need the guidance of professionals. Doctors, hospitals, health clinics, and health-related agencies all have information about local stop-smoking programs. As part of the tobacco settlement, each state now has a toll-free phone number for those looking to quit. Some are linked in with a national quitline (1-800-QUIT-NOW),

FDA BANS NICOTINE PRODUCTS

The Federal Drug Administration (FDA) must approve every drug-related product sold to consumers, including nicotine patches and gums. Many former smokers credit patches and other anti-nicotine products with helping them quit, but some products designed to help smokers quit their nicotine habit have either been blocked or banned by the FDA for their potentially dangerous uses.

A product called NicoWater was created for smokers who are accustomed to lighting up in social situations, including bars. It was pulled from shelves in 2002 when it was advertised as a dietary supplement, which was in direct violation of FDA rules. Each half-liter bottle of NicoWater had 4 milligrams of nicotine, which is about the same as two cigarettes. Unlike cigarettes and nicotine gums, however, this water was designed to taste like water and provide a source of nicotine to smokers in non-smoking environments, such as airplanes.

The FDA also banned lollipops and lip balms laced with nicotine in 2002. These products combined natural flavorings and sweeteners with a form of nicotine. They became popular with former smokers because they tasted good and eating lollipops has the same hand-to-mouth motion people use when smoking cigarettes. Pharmacists created these products as an alternative to the existing quit aids on the market today, but many people saw the lollipops as a threat to children who cannot tell the difference between ordinary treats and those that feature nicotine.

(continues on page 92)

(continued from page 91)

While NicoWater was being sold over-the-counter as a dietary supplement, some pharmacies were also selling these products online without a doctor's approval. These products' widespread availability, along with a lack of prominent warning labels on the products, helped prompt the FDA to ban their sale.

though some states have their own numbers. Teletypewriter (TTY) and multiple languages are available at http://www.naquitline.org.

Doctors can prescribe medicines to help smokers quit. Most of them release small amounts of nicotine—less than a smoker would get from a cigarette. This helps ease the discomfort of withdrawal. The medicines come in five forms: gum, patch, inhaler, nasal spray, and pill. Adults can buy some of these in drug stores without a prescription. Teenagers should talk with a health care provider before using them.

Embrace Change

Quitting is a big change. Achieving that big change requires a lot of small changes. Some of these changes might prove difficult. Smokers must alter their habits and routines. Someone who smokes with friends at lunch should make new lunch plans. If boredom triggers smoking, make sure that there is plenty to do. Avoid foods and locations that set off cravings.

Smoking is a way of rewarding the body. That reward system has to be replaced. This part of quitting can be fun. Some ex-smokers save up the money they once spent on cigarettes and use it to buy clothes or a meal at a restaurant. Find a favorite non-fattening food and eat it as a treat for staying off cigarettes.

Smokers also use cigarettes to deal with stress. When they decide to quit smoking, they must find other ways to burn off steam and relax. Shoot hoops at a neighborhood park or go jogging. Take a hot bath. Find a hobby that keeps one's hands busy, such as gardening or woodworking.

WHAT TO EXPECT

Some people can stop smoking and not feel any symptoms of withdrawal from nicotine. Most ex-smokers are not so lucky. Withdrawal symptoms usually begin within a few hours after the last cigarette and peak about two to three days later. These symptoms might last a few days or a few weeks. They include:

- Dizziness (usually gone after one or two days)
- Depression
- Feelings of frustration and anger
- Irritability
- Trouble sleeping, including trouble falling asleep and nightmares
- Inability to concentrate
- Restlessness
- Headache
- Tiredness
- Increased appetite

Watch for Relapses

Take this effort to quit smoking seriously. When cravings hit, wait 10 minutes before reaching for a cigarette. In that time, try to review all of the reasons for quitting. Remember that taking one puff or smoking one cigarette does not mean one should give up altogether.

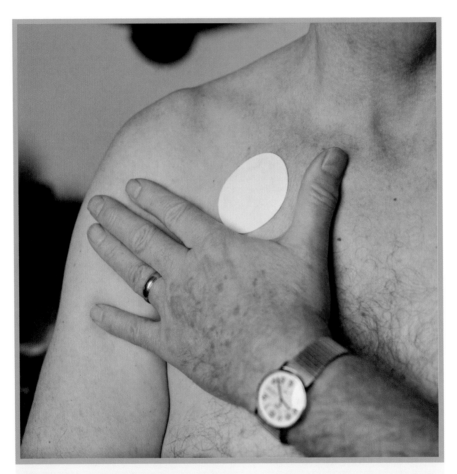

Because cigarettes contain nicotine, a highly addictive stimulant, people who try to quit smoking often start again, despite experiencing an improvement in their health. Here, a man applies a nicotine patch, which is designed to minimize the nicotine withdrawal he experiences as he attempts to quit.

On the other hand, keep in mind that most people try several times before they successfully quit smoking. If one quit attempt doesn't work, don't be discouraged. Think about what worked and what did not, and look forward to the next time around.

THE PAYOFF FOR QUITTING
With the hassle of quitting come tremendous benefits:

- After one day, your heart and blood-pressure rates improve.
- After one to nine months, coughing and shortness of breath decrease as your lungs heal.
- After two to three months, your circulation improves.
- After one year, your risk of heart disease is half of a smoker's risk.
- After 5 to 15 years, your risk of stroke is now the same as the risk of someone who has never smoked.
- After 10 years, your risk of lung cancer is half of a smoker's risk.
- After 15 years, your overall risk of dying is about the same as the risk of someone who has never smoked.

Quitting also halts the premature wrinkling of the skin and helps reduce the threat of gum disease. The sense of smell returns. Foods taste better and pleasant odors register in the brain. Climbing stairs or pushing a lawnmower can be done without gasping for breath.

CHRONOLOGY

6,000–5,000 B.C.	Organized tobacco growing probably begins among Native Americans.
1492	Christopher Columbus brings back tobacco seeds and leaves after his first voyage to the New World.
1560	French diplomat Jean Nicot sends tobacco plants to the French court, recommending them as a cure-all medicine. The word *nicotine* comes from his name.
1586	Smoking tobacco—or "sotweed"—becomes a fad in England, thanks to efforts to spread the habit by Sir Walter Raleigh and Virginia colonists.
1590–1600	European traders and missionaries introduce smoking to Korea and Japan.
1602	The English colony of Virginia raises its first commercial tobacco crop. Tobacco soon becomes the biggest money-making crop for colonial farmers.
1604	King James I of England slams smoking as unhealthy and immoral.
1614	Seville, Spain, becomes the world center for cigar production. Street beggars roll tobacco from used cigars in paper scraps, creating an early kind of cigarette.
1619	The first 20 African slaves to land in America arrive at Jamestown, Virginia. They are needed to plant and harvest tobacco.
1660	Sniffing snuff becomes popular with European royalty, replacing pipe smoking as the tobacco use of choice.

1760	Pierre Lorillard sets up the first American tobacco company (to produce pipe tobacco) in New York City.
1775–1782	Tobacco helps to fund the American Revolution against Great Britain. Tobacco crops serve as the collateral for French loans to the revolutionaries. After the war, Americans use tobacco to repay war debts.
1790s	Scientists begin to report that tobacco users face an increased risk of cancer.
1794	U.S. government imposes the first federal excise tax on tobacco. The tax targets snuff, which is used mainly by rich people. Other tobacco products remain untaxed.
1826	Cigars become increasingly popular in London. The fad spreads to other countries.
1828	German scientists isolate nicotine as being the active ingredient in tobacco. They conclude that pure nicotine is a deadly poison.
1830s	First serious anti-smoking campaign begins in the United States. Opposition to smoking is based more on moral grounds than on health concerns.
1832	An Egyptian artilleryman in Turkey officially invents the first modern cigarette. His pipe was broken, so he rolled tobacco in paper that was supposed to be used to hold gunpowder.
1839	U.S. farmers discover a way to cure tobacco that makes it milder to smoke. This bright leaf tobacco makes smoking more pleasant and popular.

1846–1848	U.S.–Mexican War introduces many U.S. soldiers to cigar tobacco from Spanish-speaking countries, boosting the cigar's already growing popularity.
1852	The invention of matches makes smoking more convenient.
1853–1856	During the Crimean War, British soldiers learn about cigarettes from Turkish allies. They introduce cigarette smoking to Europe and the practice spreads worldwide.
1861–1865	Smoking becomes more common during the Civil War as tobacco is given as rations to soldiers in both the North and the South. Northern soldiers find Southern tobacco sweeter and more enjoyable.
1880	James Bonsack makes a machine that can mass-produce cigarettes. Before, cigarettes had to be hand-rolled.
1881	North Carolina tobacco businessman James Buchanan "Buck" Duke uses Bonsack's machine to start making cigarettes. By 1889, Duke controls U.S. cigarette production. In 1902, he unites with British tobacco makers to make his control of the tobacco market international.
1911	The U.S. Supreme Court breaks up the Duke monopoly on tobacco. Duke's empire is broken into five companies: American Tobacco Co., R.J. Reynolds, Liggett & Meyers Tobacco Co., Lorillard, and British American Tobacco. These companies, along with Philip Morris and Brown & Williamson, would control tobacco sales in the decades to come.

1913	R.J. Reynolds introduces its Camel brand of cigarettes. It soon becomes the best-selling cigarette.
1914–1918	World War I causes popularity of cigarettes to soar. Soldiers find them cheaper and easier to use than other types of tobacco.
1924	Philip Morris introduces its Marlboro brand as a "mild" women's cigarette.
1938	The New York Academy of Medicine reports that smokers do not live as long as non-smokers.
1939–1945	Cigarette sales reach an all-time high during World War II.
1945–1955	Cigarette makers begin advertising on television, which is in its infancy. On a typical show, such as the hit *I Love Lucy*, the show's stars endorse Philip Morris cigarettes.
1949	About 50% of American men and 33% of American women smoke.
1950	Five major studies produce the first scientific evidence that smokers are more likely than others to get lung cancer.
1950–1960	Tobacco companies begin pushing filtered cigarettes to reassure the public's health worries, though filters do little to protect smokers.
1953	Revelations about the dangers of smoking cause cigarette sales to drop. Worried tobacco executives meet in New York to plan their response.
1954	Philip Morris creates the Marlboro Cowboy. By the 1970s, this ad campaign will make Marlboros the best-selling cigarette in

the United States and one of the most recognized brand names in the world.

1958   Major tobacco companies form the Tobacco Institute to be their lobbying arm in Washington, D.C. The organization specializes in attacking health claims made against tobacco.

1964   The U.S. surgeon general releases a report linking smoking and lung cancer. This landmark report becomes the foundation for all later anti-smoking efforts.

1965   The U.S. Congress passes the first laws requiring warning labels on cigarettes. This is later expanded to cigarette ads.

1968   Philip Morris launches the Virginia Slims brand. Its ad slogan, "You've come a long way, Baby," captures the new mood of independence among young women.

1970   Congress bans cigarette advertising on television and radio. The ban takes effect January 1, 1971. Also, cigar production peaks.

1971   Tobacco companies begin sponsoring sporting events, such as NASCAR races and Women's Tennis Association tournaments. Philip Morris' sponsorship of the Virginia Slims Tennis Tour continues until 1994.

1972   The surgeon general reports that secondhand smoke is a health risk for non-smokers. Secretly, tobacco companies step up efforts to cast doubt on health issues tied to smoking.

1973   The U.S. government orders all passenger airlines to create nonsmoking sections and bans smoking in airplane lavatories. This is the first nationwide restriction on smoking in a public place.

1973   Tobacco companies are barred from advertising "little cigars" on television or radio.

1975   The U.S. military stops giving cigarettes as part of rations to soldiers and sailors.

1977   The American Cancer Society holds the first Great American Smokeout.

1979   Minneapolis and St. Paul, Minn., become the first cities to ban the distribution of free sample cigarettes, a popular tobacco company promotional technique.

1981   Annual U.S. consumption of cigarettes peaks at 640 billion. Also, insurance companies begin offering discounts for nonsmokers on life insurance policies because they live longer.

1986   Congress requires health warnings on all packages of smokeless tobacco.

1988   The Liggett Group is ordered to pay Antonio Cipollone $400,000 in damages for contributing to the death of his wife, Rose, in 1984. Though the decision is later overturned, this marks the first time a tobacco company is ordered to pay money in such a lawsuit.

1988   The surgeon general releases *The Health Consequences of Smoking: Nicotine Addiction.* It is the first such report to deal only with nicotine and its impact.

1988   R.J. Reynolds launches its Joe Camel (or "Old Joe") ad campaign for Camel cigarettes. A 1991 study shows that the cartoon figure is as familiar to 6-year-olds as Mickey Mouse. Criticism that Joe appeals to children forces the company to end the campaign in 1997.

1990   The U.S. government bans smoking on all domestic airline flights of six hours or less.

1991   The U.S. Food and Drug Administration (FDA) approves a nicotine patch as a prescription drug. The patch is used by smokers to help them quit smoking.

1994   The heads of six major U.S. tobacco companies testify before Congress. They say that nicotine does not cause addiction and that their companies do not alter the amount of nicotine in cigarettes to make them more addictive. Their testimony is widely ridiculed.

1995   Documents come to light showing that cigarette maker Brown & Williamson knew years before that cigarettes are addictive and harmful to health.

1996   President Bill Clinton announces a program to prevent children and teens from using tobacco. It is the first program of its kind. Clinton also gives the FDA power to regulate tobacco as a drug. The U.S. Supreme Court overturns this decision in 2000.

1997   Lawsuits against the Liggett Group force the company to admit that smoking is addictive and can cause cancer. The company also admits that the industry markets cigarettes to teenagers.

1998   California becomes the first state to ban smoking in bars. By 2007, 37 states have passed bans on smoking in bars, restaurants, or all workplaces.

1998	Forty-six states and five U.S. territories agree to a $206 billion settlement with tobacco companies. The states filed lawsuits to recoup healthcare costs tied to tobacco use.
2003	A new law bans new tobacco sponsorships, advertising on billboards and in the press, and the free distribution of cigarettes. Tobacco companies also cannot use direct mail, the Internet, or other new types of promotions to entice people to use their products.
2005	The United States begins phasing out subsidies to tobacco farmers. The subsidies began in the 1930s to help small farmers. Without subsidies, tobacco growing becomes less profitable. U.S. tobacco production, which was already declining, drops sharply.
2007	The Motion Picture Association of America agrees to consider the presence of tobacco products as a factor in determining the ratings for movies.

GLOSSARY

Addiction   A compulsive need for a habit-forming substance. The need can be physiological, psychological or both, as is the case with nicotine.

Adrenaline   A chemical in the body that is stimulated by nicotine. Adrenaline, which is also called epinephrine, speeds up the heart rate and breathing.

Bidis   (*bee-dees*) Thin, hand-rolled cigarettes that originated in India. Their tobacco is often laced with candy flavors that are popular with teenagers.

Bright leaf   A type of tobacco (also called flue-cured or Virginia tobacco) that is cured, or dried, using artificial heat from pipes, or flues.

Burley   A type of air-cured, or dried, tobacco used in cigarettes.

Cancer   An abnormal growth of cells in the body that can spread, causing illness and death.

Chewing tobacco   Flavored tobacco that is put in the mouth between the cheek and gum.

Cigars   Cut tobacco leaves that are rolled within other tobacco leaves into tube shapes and smoked.

Cigarette   A paper tube filled with chopped up tobacco that is smoked. Most cigarettes today also have filters made of fiber or charcoal designed to cut down on the number of dangerous chemicals reaching the lungs.

Dopamine   A chemical in the brain tied to pleasure. Nicotine stimulates dopamine production. This gives a tobacco user a brief, comforting sensation but also intensifies his or her dependence upon nicotine.

Hookah   A type of water pipe. The smoke passes through a vessel of water before it reaches the smoker, making it less harsh on the lungs.

Kreteks   (*creh-teks*) Clove cigarettes from Indonesia that are popular with teenagers.

Menthol   A type of alcohol used as an additive in tobacco to give it a minty flavor.

Nicotine   A highly addictive drug found in tobacco plants that stimulates both the heart rate and the brain's pleasure centers. In concentrated form, nicotine is a poison.

Oriental   A type of sun-dried tobacco grown mainly in Asia and often used in conjunction with other tobaccos in U.S. cigarettes.

Pipe   A tube with a mouthpiece on one end and a bowl on the other. Tobacco held in the bowl is burned, and the fumes are breathed in through the mouthpiece.

Plug   A small, tightly packed cake of flavored tobacco that is usually used for chewing.

Second hand smoke   The smoke from a tobacco product that is either exhaled from the smoker's lungs or excess "side-stream" smoke that is unused by the smoker.

Snuff   A form of powdered tobacco that is either sniffed up the nose or "dipped" between the cheek and gum.

Surgeon general   The leader of the U.S. Public Health Service.

Tar   The residue of tobacco smoke, much of which settles in the lungs of a smoker. Tar is made up of many different chemicals.

Tax   A government fee for a good or service. Tobacco products are heavily taxed.

Tobacco   Any of several plants belonging to the genus *Nicotiana* whose leaves are consumed by smoking, chewing, or sniffing.

BIBLIOGRAPHY

BOOKS

Balkin, Karen and Helen Cothran, eds. *Tobacco and Smoking: Opposing Viewpoints*. San Diego, Calif.: Greenhaven Press, 2004.

Brandt, Allan M. *The Cigarette Century: The Rise, Fall, and Deadly Persistence of the Product that Defined America*. New York: Basic Books, 2007.

Eriksen, Michael, Judith Mackay, and Omar Shafey. *The Tobacco Atlas, 2nd ed*. Atlanta, Ga.: American Cancer Society, 2006.

Glantz, Stanton A., et al. *The Cigarette Papers*. Berkeley, Calif.: University of California Press, 1996.

Goodman, Jordan. *Tobacco in History and Culture: An Encyclopedia*. Farmington Hills, Mich.: Thomson Gale, 2005.

Hirschfelder, Arlene B. *Encyclopedia of Smoking and Tobacco*. Phoenix, Ariz.: Oryx Press, 1999.

MacDonald, Joan V. *Tobacco and Nicotine: Drug Dangers*. Berkeley Heights, N.J.: Enslow, 2001.

Parker-Pope, Tara. *Cigarettes: Anatomy of an Industry from Seed to Smoke*. New York: The New Press, 2001.

Tate, Cassandra. *Cigarette Wars: The Triumph of the "Little White Slaver."* New York: Oxford University Press, 1999.

Taylor, Peter. *The Smoke Ring: Tobacco, Money, and Multinational Politics*. New York: Pantheon Books, 1984.

U.S. Dept. of Health and Human Services. *Preventing Tobacco Use Among Young People: A Report of the Surgeon General*. Atlanta, Ga.: U.S. Dept. of Health and Human Services, Public Health Service, Centers for Disease Control and Prevention, National Center for Chronic Disease Prevention and Health Promotion, Office on Smoking and Health, 1994.

Wagner, Heather Lehr. *Nicotine*. Philadelphia, Penn.: Chelsea House Publishers, 2003.

Zegart, Dan. *Civil Warriors: The Legal Siege on the Tobacco Industry*. New York: Delacourte Press, 2000.

ARTICLES

"Anti-smoking 'Truth' Campaign Helped Slash Youth Smoking Rates, Study Says." Associated Press (February 22, 2005).

Associated Press. "Some Nicotine-laced Water Pulled From Stores." CNN Web site. http://www.cnn.com/2004/HEALTH/01/09/nicotine.water.ap/index.html.

Associated Press. "Nicotine-spiked Lollipops, Lip Balm Illegal, FDA Says." USA Today Web site. http://www.usatoday.com/news/health/smoking/2002–04–11-nicotine-lollipops.htm.

"Attorney General Blumenthal, 39 States Praise Proposed Rules to Halt Mislabeling of Cigarettes as 'Little Cigars,'" U.S. Fed News Service. Available online. URL: http://www.time.com/time/europe/magazine/2003/0113/cover/story.html.

Bakalar, Nicholas. "Nicotine Addiction Is Quick In Youths, Research Finds." *The New York Times* Web site. URL: www.nytimes.com/2007/07/31/health/31toba.html.

Cieply, Michael. "Puffing Away That PG Rating." *The New York Times* (May 11, 2007).

Johnston, D.C. and Warner, M. "Tobacco Makers Lose Key Ruling on Latest Suits." *The New York Times* Web site. URL: www.nytimes.com/2006/09/26/business/26tobacco.html.

Landers, Susan J. "Congress Again Tries to Give FDA Control Over Tobacco." *American Medical News* (March 19, 2007).

Lewis, Libby. "Analysis: Judge, Citing Reservations, Backs Anti-tobacco Ads." National Public Radio (August 23, 2005).

Mackay, J. and Eriksen, M. "The Tobacco Atlas." World Health Organization Web site. URL: www.who.int/tobacco/resources/publications/tobacco_atlas/en/.

Mayhew, K.P., B.R. Flay, and J.A. Mott, "Stages in the Development of Adolescent Smoking." *Drug and Alcohol Dependence* 59, Supp. 1 (2000): S61-S81.

Mozes, Alan. "First Puff Can Turn Kids Into Smokers: Study." Healthfinder.gov Web site. URL: www.healthfinder.gov/news/newsstory.asp?docID=608677.

"People Who Smoke Light Cigarettes Are Less Likely To Quit." University of Pittsburgh Medical Center Web site. URL: www.upmc.com/Communications/MediaRelations/Research/Articles/LightCigarettes.htm.

Sohn, Pam. "Hanging Up the Last Leaves to Dry: Farmer Drops Unprofitable Tobacco Crop." *Chattanooga Times Free Press* (May 1, 2007).

Stobbe, Mike. "75% of U.S. Households Forbid Smoking, Study Finds." Associated Press (May 25, 2007).

"The Truth About 'Light' Cigarettes: Q&A." National Cancer Institute Web site. URL: www.cancer.gov/cancertopics/factsheet/Tobacco/light-cigarettes.

"Treating Tobacco Use and Dependence," United States Department of Health and Human Services, Agency for Healthcare Research and Quality. URL: www.ahrq.gov/path/tobacco.htm.

White, Gayle. "Expert: Curb Film Smoking, Aid Teens." Cox News Service (October 12, 2006).

"Why Is Tobacco a Public Health Priority?" World Health Organization. URL: www.who.int/tobacco/en.

WEB SITES

American Cancer Society. URL: www.cancer.org

American Heart Association. URL: www.americanheart.org

American Lung Association. URL: www.lungusa.org

"Building a World Where Young People Reject Tobacco and Anyone Can Quit," American Legacy Foundation. URL: www.americanlegacy.org

Campaign for Tobacco Free Kids. URL: http://tobaccofreekids.org

"Independence from Smoking: A Breath of Fresh Air!" U.S. Department of Health and Human Services. URL: www.4woman.gov/quitsmoking/teens

Nicotine Anonymous. URL: www.nicotine-anonymous.org

Nicotine Free Kids. URL: www.nicotinefreekids.org

The Oral Cancer Foundation. URL: www.oralcancerfoundation.org

"Prevention Online," Alcohol and Drug Information. Substance Abuse and Mental Heath Services Administration of the U.S. Department of Health and Human Services. URL: http://ncadi.samhsa.gov

QuitNet: Quit All Together. URL: www.quitnet.org

"Smoking and Tobacco Use," U.S. Department of Health and Human Services: Centers for Disease Control and Prevention. URL: www.cdc.gov/tobacco

Society for Research on Nicotine and Tobacco. URL: www.srnt.org

"Tobacco Cessation—You Can Quit Smoking Now!" U.S. Department of Health and Human Services. URL: www.surgeongeneral.gov/tobacco

Tobacco Control Archives. Galen Digital Library. University of California, San Francisco. URL: www.library.ucsf.edu/tobacco

"Tobacco News and Information," tobacco.org. URL: www.tobacco.org

United States Department of Health and Human Services, National Institutes of Health, National Cancer Institute. URL: www.cancer.gov

"You Can Quit Smoking Now!" Smokefree.gov. URL: www.smokefree.gov

FURTHER READING

BOOKS

American Lung Association. *How to Quit Smoking Without Gaining Weight.* New York: Pocket Books, 2004.

Goodman, Jordan. *Tobacco in History and Culture: An Encyclopedia.* Farmington Hills, Mich.: Thomson Gale, 2005.

Kluger, Richard. *Ashes to Ashes.* New York: Alfred A. Knopf, 1996.

MacDonald, Joan V. *Tobacco and Nicotine: Drug Dangers.* Berkeley Heights, N.J.: Enslow, 2001.

Parker-Pope, Tara. *Cigarettes: Anatomy of an Industry from Seed to Smoke.* New York: The New Press, 2001.

WEB SITES

THE AMERICAN CANCER SOCIETY

This site presents a wealth of information on cancer. Search its facts & figures page to learn more about specific cancers. Also, read about the latest medical innovations to fight the disease, as well as ways to support cancer research in your community.

http://www.cancer.org

THE AMERICAN HEART ASSOCIATION

Gain valuable information on heart disease and prevention at this Web site. Read true-life stories of people who have dealt with and overcome heart disease and learn what you can do to maintain a healthy heart. Shop at their online stores to support heart research.

http://www.americanheart.org

CAMPAIGN FOR TOBACCO-FREE KIDS

Read about the latest efforts of a progressive campaign to inform the world of the negative impact of smoking. Learn of state and federal initiatives to help kids and adults understand the damaging effects of tobacco, cigarettes, and secondhand smoke.

http://tobaccofreekids.org

CENTERS FOR DISEASE CONTROL AND PREVENTION

The U.S. Centers for Disease Control and Prevention is part of the Department of Health and Human Services. The site presents detailed information on tobacco and its harmful health effects. Read about tobacco prevention and ways to quit.

http://www.cdc.gov/tobacco

CURRENT INFORMATION ON TOBACCO

Search this informed resource on tobacco and smoking for current world issues regarding these topics. Use the search tools to browse tobacco information related to the United States, as well as international communities.

http://www.tobacco.org

THE NATIONAL CANCER INSTITUTE

This institute is part of the National Institutes of Health, the primary federal agency for medical research. Find the latest information on specific cancers and the current treatment options for this disease. A section of the site is devoted to smoking, its negative impact on health, and ways to quit.

http://www.cancer.gov

THE NATIONAL INSTITUTE ON DRUG ABUSE

The National Institutes of Health focuses on tobacco issues through the National Institute on Drug Abuse. The NIDA Web site offers valuable information about tobacco use, including a section on tobacco and teens.

http://smoking.drugabuse.gov/

THE NATIONAL INSTITUTES OF HEALTH

The NIH also offers a helpful Web site on nicotine-related topics. Much of it is dedicated to efforts to stop smoking.

http://health.nih.gov/result.asp/607

NATIONAL WOMAN'S HEALTH INFORMATION CENTER

Check out this area of a site targeted to women, which includes information for teens who smoke or are thinking of starting. The site also provides several links to publications and other Internet resources that deal with teen smoking.

http://www.4woman.gov/quitsmoking/teens

SMOKE FREE MOVIES

Go to this site of the University of California, San Francisco's campaign to stamp out smoking in youth-oriented films. Read about the campaign's initiatives, and information related to smoking and the U.S. film industry.

http://smokefreemovies.ucsf.edu

THE TOBACCO ATLAS, 2ND EDITION

This online version of the American Cancer Society's *The Tobacco Atlas, 2nd Edition*, is an in-depth resource on tobacco, its effects on society, the world economy, and health.

http://www.cancer.org/docroot/AA/content/AA_2_5_9x_Tobacco_Atlas.asp

VIDEO VAULT: OLD TV ADS

Take a look at the cigarette industry's past. View old television advertisements that promoted cigarette use. Gain a deeper understanding of the tobacco industry's impact and influence on supporting the early days of television.

http://www.tvparty.com/vaultcomcig.html

WORLD HEALTH ORGANIZATION

The World Health Organization is the world's premier voice
on international health and disease. Check out this site
to view tobacco-related information and initiatives of this
prominent organization, as well as worldwide actions to
lessen tobacco use.

http://www.who.int/tobacco/en

PHOTO CREDITS

INDEX

A

addiction
  as chemical dependence, 13
  how nicotine works, 67–70
  Massachusetts study on,
    78–79
  quitting and, 86
  tobacco company
    knowledge of, 48
  withdrawal symptoms, 93
additives, 65–66
adrenaline, 68
advertising
  anti-smoking ads, 83–85
  ban on TV cigarette ads, 45
  product placements, 38–40
  young people and, 81–83
airlines, 47
alkaloids, 67–68
Altria, 66
American Cancer Society, 89
American Heart Association,
  89
American Legacy Foundation,
  83, 85
American Lung Association, 89
American Tobacco Co., 33
anti-smoking ads, 83–85
anti-smoking movements
  advertisements and, 83
  movies and, 40
  secondhand smoke and,
    45–48
  smokers' rights and, 51
  World War I and, 33–34
anti-smoking programs, 49
appearance, 72–73, 87
authority, bucking, 78–79
average smoke, 15–18

B

Baby Boomers, 40
Bacall, Lauren, 38

baseball, 59–60
baseball cards, 32
bidis, 55
Bonsack, James, 33
breaking the habit. *See*
  quitting
bright leaf tobacco, 28, 64
British American Tobacco,
  33, 66
Brown & Williamson, 38,
  66, 82
Bull Durham tobacco, 59
Burley tobacco, 64

C

Camel cigarettes, 83
Campaign for Tobacco-Free
  Kids, 89
cancer
  cigars and, 56–57
  research on tobacco and,
    37, 42
  Surgeon General's report,
    44
cardiovascular conditions, 73
cellulose acetate, 54
Centers for Disease Control
  and Prevention (CDC),
  13, 90
chemicals in tobacco
  smoke, 69
chewing tobacco, 29, 58–61
children, 37, 75
China National Tobacco
  Company, 66
Cigar Aficionado magazine, 51,
  55–56
cigarettes
  advertising for, 45
  bidis and kreteks, 55
  as "drug delivery system,"
    13, 53–55
  filtered, 42, 54–55

cigarettes *(continued)*
  ingredients in, 13–15
  invention and rise of, 28–33
  "light" or "low tar," 71–72
  nicotine content, 15
  warning labels, 46
cigars, 13, 15, 55–57
Cipollone, Antonio, 48
Cipollone, Rose, 48
Civil War, 28
"cold turkey," 88
Columbus, Christopher,
  22–23
cost of smoking, 87–88

D
death, 12, 75. *See also* health
  impacts
depression, 80
developing countries, 17
Dickens, Charles, 29
DiFranza, Joseph, 79
doctors, 92
dopamine, 68, 69
Duke, James Buchanan
  "Buck," 28–33

E
eating, 79–80
education and tobacco use,
  16–17
emphysema, 73
experimenting, 82

F
family, 77, 88
Fast and the Furious: Tokyo Drift
  (movie), 39
filtered cigarettes, 42, 54–55
fire safety, 25, 31
Food and Drug
  Administration, U.S. (FDA),
  51–52, 91–92

France, 23
French Revolution, 27
friends, 77–78, 88

G
Grant, Ulysses S., 57
green tobacco sickness, 64–66
gum problems, 72

H
hand-to-mouth activity, 79–80
health care costs, 20
health impacts
  cancer, 37, 42, 44, 56–57
  death, 12, 75
  how nicotine works, 67–70
  long-range problems, 73–75
  quitting and, 87
  why young smokers should
    worry, 70–73
heart disease, 73
Hemingway, Ernest, 34
history of tobacco and
  smoking
  overview, 13
  baseball cards and, 32
  chronology, 96–103
  Civil War and, 28
  European exploration and
    colonies and, 22–25
  Native Americans, 22
  rise of cigarettes, 28–33
  World War I, 33–36
  World War II, 36
  worldwide spread of, 25–28
Hollywood, 38–40
hookahs, 58

J
Jackson, Andrew, 57
Jackson, Rachel, 57
Jackson, "Shoeless" Joe, 59
Joe Camel, 83

K
kreteks, 55

L
lawsuits, 47, 48–51
Liggett & Meyers Tobacco Co., 33
Liggett Group, 48, 66
"light" cigarettes, 71–72
lip balms, 91
lollipops, 91
Lorillard, 33, 66
"low tar" cigarettes, 71–72
lung cancer. *See* cancer

M
McKinley, William, 57
men and tobacco, 16, 44
menthol, 66
metabolic rate, 80
minors, sale of tobacco to, 85
money, tobacco as, 27
Motion Picture Association of America (MPAA), 40
mouth, effects of smoking on, 72
movies, 38–40, 80–81

N
National Cancer Institute, 90
National Enquirer, 45
Native Americans
 chewing tobacco and, 58–60
 in history of tobacco, 22, 27
 number of smokers, 16
 pipes and, 57
neurotransmitters, 68
news media, 48
Nicot, Jean, 23–25
Nicotiana, 23–24, 62
Nicotiana rustica, 62
Nicotiana tabacum, 13, 62

nicotine, definition of, 13
nicotine fast facts, 19–20
NicoWater, 91, 92

O
101 Dalmatians (movie), 39
Oriental tobacco, 64

P
parents, 77
patches, 91
peer pressure, 78
Pershing, John, 34
Philip Morris, 38, 66
pipe tobacco, 13
pipes, 57–58
plugs, 61
Portugal, 23
pregnant women, 37, 75
prescription medicines, 92
presidents, U.S., 57
private homes, smoking in, 40, 48
product placements, 38–40
productivity, lost, 20
professional help quitting, 90–92
Prohibition, 34
public places, 47
public relations and tobacco companies, 41–42, 44–45

Q
quitting
 overview, 86–87
 embracing change, 92–93
 finding support, 88–90
 getting ready, 88
 payoff for, 95
 professional help, 90–92
 "quitting will be easy," 77
 reasons to quit, 87–88
 relapses, 94–95

quitting *(continued)*
   resources for help and
      information, 89–90
   withdrawal symptoms, 93

R
racial groups, 16
Raleigh, Walter, 25
reasons people smoke,
   12–13
reasons to quit, 87–88
reasons young people smoke,
   76–81
rebellion, 78–79
regulation of tobacco
   cigars and, 56
   by FDA, 51–52
   laws and restrictions,
      47–48
   warning labels and
      advertising, 45, 46
research and studies
   in 1950, 37–40
   on addiction, 78–79
   by tobacco companies, 42,
      48
reward systems, 92–93
rights of smokers, 51
R.J. Reynolds, 33, 42, 66, 76,
   83
Rocky (movie), 38
Roosevelt, Eleanor, 36
Rothmans International, 66
Ruth, Babe, 59

S
sale of tobacco to minors, 85
secondhand smoke, 19, 45–48,
   75
skin, effects of smoking on,
   72–73
smell, 87
smokeless tobaccos, 69–70

"smoker's face," 72–73
smoking. *See* cigarettes; health
   impacts; history of tobacco
   and smoking; quitting
*Smoking and Health: Report of
   the Advisory Committee to the
   Surgeon General of the Public
   Health Service,* 44
snuff, 13, 27, 61
social acceptance and
   quitting, 87
Spain, 23
speakeasies, 34
spitting and spittoons, 29
steps to becoming a
   smoker, 82
stress, 80, 93
suicide, 80
Sun Also Rises, The
   (Hemingway), 34
Superman II (movie), 38
Surgeon General, U.S., 18–19,
   42–44, 47–48
Surgeon General's Warning, 46

T
tar, 54
taste of tobacco, 14–15
taxes, 28, 47, 87–88
Taylor, Peter, 12
teenagers and smoking, 18–21,
   40
Terry, Luther L., 42–44
To Have and Have Not (movie),
   38
tobacco. *See also* history of
   tobacco and smoking
   basics on the plant, 61–63
   bright leaf, 28, 64
   Burley, 64
   as money, 27
   Nicotiana tabacum, 13
   Oriental, 64